CAMARO

Steve Statham

MBI Publishing Company

First published in 1998 by MBI Publishing Company,
729 Prospect Avenue, PO Box 1, Osceola, WI 54020-0001
USA

MBI Publishing Company books are also available at
discounts in bulk quantity for industrial or sales-promotional
use. For details write to Special Sales Manager at
Motorbooks International Wholesalers & Distributors, 729
Prospect Avenue, Osceola, WI 54020-0001 USA.

Library of Congress Cataloging-in-Publication Data

Statham, Steve.
    Camaro/Steve Statham.
            p. cm.--(Muscle car color history)
    Includes index.
    ISBN 0-7603-0426-2 (pbk.: alk. paper)
    1. Camaro automobile--History. I. Title. II. Series:
muscle car color history.
TL215.C33S73   1998
629.222'2--dc21   98-23725

On the front cover: Pictured is a 1969 SS396 Rally Sport
convertible owned by Harry Hylkema of Redlands,
California. *Steve Statham*

On the back cover: In 1993, the Camaro came back with a
vengeance. This teaser photo was used by Chevrolet to let the
enthusiasts know that a new model was in the works.
Steve Statham

Designed by Rebecca Allen

Printed in Hong Kong

Contents

Acknowledgments

For those of us of a certain age, a 1969 Camaro was the coolest set of wheels a high-schooler could possibly own. Even better, a 1969 Z28 was enough to immortalize a teen forever in high school legend, or would have been if anyone at our school had been fortunate enough to own one. But any Camaro carried enough weight in our street-machine glory days to earn the respect of high-school peers. In 1977 the Z28 was reintroduced, and a previously low-profile semi-geek at school was instantly transformed into a semi-cool dude upon his acquisition of the first new Z in our area—I leave the "semi" in here because his dad did buy it for him, and he ordered the car with an automatic.

Lots of other people have memories of Camaro glory, and many of those glories happened far beyond the insular walls of high school. The Camaro has been a special car to a wide range of people for a lot of different reasons. Even after 32 years (as this is written) Camaros still generate warm and fuzzy memories across the land in young and old alike. The car is remembered for spectacular racing exploits, thrilling Sunday drives, clandestine street races, intensive customizing projects, even great battles waged high in the towers of the business world.

Hopefully, this book will keep some of those memories preserved for a long time. With that in mind, I'd like to thank those photographers, experts, and enthusiasts who contributed to this project. First thanks go to good friend Mike Mueller, whose photography of Paul McGuire's two 1967 Z28s, Felix and Barbara Lopez's 1967 Nickey Camaro, Milton Robson's 1968 Dana Camaro, Mick Price's 1969 427 COPO Camaro, and Dick Hubbard's 1969 ZL-1 Camaro really helped dress up this book. Another good friend, Tom Wilson, gave me room and board during my great California Camaro photo safari and let me rummage through his office library; he deserves a place near the top of the mention list. My brother Jeff and his wife Jennifer also offered excellent (free) lodging during my many excursions to Denver. Thanks, bro.

Bird-doggin' thanks are offered to Bob Brennan with the Cool Runnin' Camaros in Southern California and the Michels with the Camaro Club of San Diego. These car club leaders were tremendously helpful in recommending cars for me to photograph, and their opinions were always right on target. Gregg Cly at Mustang, Muscle & More in Dallas gets a big *gracias* for always cheerfully tossing me the keys to the nicer Camaros that passed through his dealership.

Mega-thanks to Greg Rager and Donald Farr at Dobbs Publishing Group, who graciously cracked open the Roger Huntington photo archives for use in this book. Greg, the last person to interview Don Yenko before his untimely demise in 1987, also went the extra mile and contributed photography from his Yenko collection, and this book is much better for it.

Also deserving of gratitude are Mark Patrick with the Detroit Public Library National Automotive History Collection, Barry Kluczyk at *Pro* magazine, and Bob Plumer with Drag Racing Memories (200 N. Kalmia Ave., Highland Springs, VA 23075) for his help in securing vintage drag racing photos. Bob Tronolone also contributed some wonderful vintage racing photography.

Thanks also to those who risked phoner's ear by sitting for interviews, specifically Reg Harris with SLP engineering, Joel Rosen with Baldwin Performance, and Chuck Hughes for

The grille and hood of a 1969 SS-350 equipped with the Z10 Indy Pace Car Coupe option.

our marathon Chevy II/Camaro session. (And Trans-Am racer Dorsey Schroeder, some of whose pre-Dallas Grand Prix remarks from 1994 are included herein. We were talking Fords at the time, but the Camaro versus Mustang comparisons were irresistible.) Baldwin/Motion historian Tim Penton Jr. (1108 W. Thomas St., Hammond, LA 70401) also helped me gather material and deserves thanks.

I'd be remiss if I didn't acknowledge the valuable insights and information provided by writers who have trod this ground before me. Particularly valuable texts included: *Camaro! From Challenger to Champion: The Complete History* by Gary Witzenburg, the *Camaro White Book* by Mike Antonick, *Trans-Am Racing, 1966–1985* by Albert Bochroch, and the *Standard Catalog of Chevrolet 1912–1990* by Pat Chappell.

Finally, I must warmly thank the car owners who graciously allowed me to photograph their Camaros for use in this book.

These owners are, in basic order of appearance: Larry Christensen, Arvada, CO, 1967 Indy Pace Car convertible, 1969 Yenko 427, 1969 Indy Pace Car convertible, and 1997 Brickyard 400 convertible; Donald and Tracie Robles, San Jacinto, CA, 1967 Sport Coupe six-cylinder; Ricky Ratliff, Emory, TX, 1967 SS/RS-350; Jim Michelson, Riverside, CA, 1968 convertible; Jim Weil, Fountain Valley, CA, 1969 Z28 Rally Sport; Ronnie McEnturff, Emory, TX, 1969 Z-10 Pace Car Coupe; Dave Swisher, Austin, TX, 1969 Z28 cross ram; Harry Hylkema, Redlands, CA, 1969 SS-396 Rally Sport convertible; Carl Virden, Stanton, CA, 1969 SS-350; Gregg Cly's Mustang, Muscle & More, Dallas, TX, 1970 SS-396 and 1970 Z28; Mrs. T. R. Hartsell and Gary Hartsell, El Cajon, CA, 1973 Rally Sport; and the unknown owner of the supercharged 1968 Camaro street machine from that long-ago Florida car show. Thanks, all.

The Camaro has a long and rich history, but the 1969 version (especially the Z/28) is one of the all-time favorites.

While the Indy Pace Car convertible version of the 1969 Camaro is a well-known and sought-after model, a few Camaro coupes slipped out the door with Indy Pace Car accents but no pace car decals.

1

In the Beginning . . .

It must have been frustrating for Chevrolet engineers, stylists, and planners. Here it was, 1964, and Chevrolet built not only the most technically sophisticated car in America—the Corvette—but the most technically daring sporty compact—the Corvair—plus the powerful Chevelle Malibu Super Sport. Yet what were America's youths doing? Frantically waving money at Ford dealers in desperate attempts to be the first on the block to own a new Mustang, a car that was little more than a Falcon with stylish sheet metal. *Time* and *Newsweek* were heaping lavish coverage on the new car, and Lee Iacocca was becoming a minor celebrity.

General Motors may have ruled the world, but it clearly did not rule the sporty coupe market in the mid-1960s—which must have been galling to people who were *sure* they were producing superior automobiles. The Ford Falcon had already posted better sales numbers than the unique Corvair, and then this: 121,538 Mustangs built in the abbreviated first four months of production and 559,451 Mustangs produced for the 1965 model year alone!

With this cold splash of reality, the seeds for the Camaro were planted. Nobody likes to play catch-up, but Chevrolet decision makers suddenly found themselves in the position of creating a new car that would inevitably be defined by how well it out-Mustanged the Mustang. So, like David and Goliath, IBM and Macintosh, or the Dallas Cowboys and Washington Redskins, it is inevitable in the case of the Chevrolet Camaro that its history will be forever linked to that of its main rival—Ford's Mustang. Doubtless, scores of Chevy partisans will bristle at the suggestion, but you can't discuss the Camaro without talking about Ford's Mustang. The Camaro exists because of the Mustang's success.

In giving the Mustang its due, it's no exaggeration to say it was an automobile that completely altered the American performance car landscape. Until then, American manufacturers had not quite found the middle ground between large-ish, two-door sedans and tiny imported sports cars. Although thoroughly conventional under the skin, the Mustang's combination of sporty looks, compact size, decent performance, and low price made it an instant, smashing success. The Mustang introduced young Americans to the now famous long hood/short deck proportions and the term "ponycar."

Not that any of the above should diminish the late-arriving Camaro in any way. The Mustang may have been first, but the Camaro has usually been faster, nearly always handled better, and has definitely been the more stylish choice. Chevrolet never devalued the Camaro by creating a shrunken economy-car trading on the great name, as Ford did with the Mustang II. For more than 30 years the Camaro has been Chevrolet's affordable performance car, and for many of those years the best performance car buy in the United States.

For slightly more than the price of a mundane GM sedan, the Camaro has offered style and performance that has rivaled that of mega-dollar foreign exoticars. There have been Z28s, Super Sports, Rally Sports, Indy Pace Cars, IROC-Zs, and others. Although the Corvette has always led the Chevy pack, there have been many years when the Camaro offered 90 percent of the Corvette's abilities for half the price. Often

A one-year body style, the 1969 Camaro remains one of the favorites among collectors. It was also popular when new—the 1969 model was the best-seller of the first-generation cars. Shown is an SS-396 Rally Sport convertible, one of 17,573 convertibles built that year. The 1969s were the last Camaro convertibles until 1987, when ASC-modified droptops rejoined the lineup. In 1969, a convertible top added about $200 to the sticker price; in 1987, the premium was more than $4,000.

General Motors conducted wind-tunnel tests using a quarter-scale Camaro model to track the new car's aerodynamic properties. Dots of ink left trails along the body when subjected to high wind speeds, revealing to engineers how air flowed over the body. *Roger Huntington Collection/ Dobbs Publishing Group*

styling vice president Bill Mitchell. They quietly worked on mock-ups and proposals for a sporty coupe, using the just-introduced Chevy II as a base.

The 1962 idea was slapped down by the higher-ups. (Chevrolet already had four successful, separate car lines, with a fifth, the Chevelle, under development.) But the concept didn't completely go away. The Super Nova show car introduced at the 1964 New York Auto Show incorporated many of the characteristics proposed earlier and raised some eyebrows at the show. But Chevrolet was doing well without a specialized coupe, and GM management saw no need to augment the line-up with a sporty two-door.

Then came the Mustang, with its blizzard of publicity and army of buyers. GM decision makers may have been puzzled by the Mustang's popular appeal, but the market's response to the car taught them it was a winning formula. In late 1964, the decision was made to start work on a competitor for the Mustang. It was scheduled for introduction in the fall of 1966.

This new car was given an internal code of XP-836. Outside GM, mostly in the media, the car was referred to as the "Panther," one

the top-of-the-line Camaro was a more entertaining car than an entry-level Corvette.

And besides, the Camaro nearly beat the Mustang out of the gate. Many inside Chevrolet had been kicking around the idea of such a car since at least 1962. That's when Irv Rybicki, then Chevrolet chief designer, had discussed the concept with GM

The Z28 debuted in 1967, and what a debut it was. Roger Penske and Mark Donohue quickly took the Z28 to victory in SCCA Trans-Am competition, winning the manufacturers' championship the following year. Although the Z28 started off low-key in the marketplace, it quickly established a following. Only 602 were built the first year, but by 1969 the number ballooned to 20,302. *Detroit Public Library National Automotive History Collection*

of the names known to be under consideration for the final product. Henry Haga, head of Chevrolet Styling Studio Number 2, was given primary responsibility for the new car's styling. George Angersbach was tasked with making the interior appropriately sporty (and economical to manufacture). Don McPherson was chief engineer for engines and passenger car transmissions at the time. Semon E. "Bunkie" Knudsen was Chevrolet general manager at the beginning of the program, although he moved up the corporate hierarchy in 1965. Pete Estes was Chevrolet general manager during the Camaro's final development and launch.

The Camaro was one of the earliest cars to benefit from the intense use of computers in the development process. Also influencing the Camaro's final form was the shared platform with a revamped 1968 Chevy II. This knowledge gave savvy magazine and newspaper editors an insight into the "Panther's" final form, although it was an insight that usually turned out to be inaccurate.

In a *Car Life* road test of the 1966 Nova SS with the 350-horsepower 327-cubic inch V-8 underhood, the editors noted: "One of the least-kept secrets in Detroit is that the Chevy II is, for all practical purposes, the mechanical prototype for Chevrolet's forthcoming Panther. The test car provides vivid proof that this is a sound basis upon which to build a sporting type of car. The Chevy II 327, for example, could hold its own among all Mustangs except the Shelby GT-350. Its Corvette engine puts all lesser Mustangs in the shade, although its lack of effective brakes leaves an important plus in the opposition camp's disc brake option."

Of course, the 1967 Camaro never offered the L79 327 that so impressed the *Car Life* staff, but it did debut the 350-cubic inch small-block V-8 and the Z28's high-revving 302 V-8, perhaps the two most famous versions of Chevrolet's timeless V-8. What the Camaro and 1968 Chevy II/Nova did share, though, was a semi-unibody main structure with a bolt-on front subframe. This design was intended to offer better isolation of the drivetrain from the passenger compartment, along with providing advantages during the assembly process. The Camaro also shared the single-leaf "Monoplate" rear springs of the Chevy II, which many would later blame for assorted traction-related headaches in performance-model Camaros. The single-leaf springs did not last long; by 1968 they were used only on the entry-level Camaros,

as the cars with larger V-8s switched to multi-leaf rear springs.

As for the name Camaro, it is derived from a French word for friend, although it had less-friendly connotations when pronounced in other European languages. The decision on the name came down to the last minute, with most of the world sure the car was to be introduced as the Panther. Although the strange name had to be explained to the press and public, Camaro fit in with the other C-names in the Chevy line-up: Corvette, Chevelle, Chevy II, and Corvair.

The Camaro arrived on the scene with a score of Mustang-beaters in the fall of 1966, including a styled Plymouth Barracuda and Mercury's new Cougar. More ponycars would come later, as nearly every auto maker scrambled for a piece of the Mustang pie. AMC threw out the Javelin for 1968. Dodge introduced the Challenger for 1970. Even newcomer Toyota offered a Japanese version of the Mustang, the Celica, for 1971. Ford execs even figured one Mustang wasn't enough and imported the "British Mustang," the Mercury Capri, for 1971.

General Motors belatedly decided to fight the Mustang on two fronts. After much dithering, Pontiac was given the go-ahead for its own version of the Panther, the Firebird (see sidebar). The Firebird had a late introduction, after most of the other 1967s had been introduced, thus giving the Camaro a head start in the Mustang war.

For its part, the Camaro was roughly the same size as the Mustang, a little wider,

The Camaro's arch-enemy, on the street and on the track, has always been the Mustang. The SCCA's Trans-Am series has especially magnified the rivalry. Ford took the championship in 1967 and 1970. Chevy dominated in 1968 and 1969. Here, Camaro ace Mark Donohue leads Dan Gurney into turn nine at Laguna Seca in August 1969. Donohue had a stellar racing career that included 29 career Trans-Am victories, 3 championships, and a victory in the 1972 Indianapolis 500. He died in an on-track accident in 1975. *Bob Tronolone*

slightly heavier, and definitely more performance-oriented. Whereas the Mustang GT offered only 289-cubic inch or under-achieving 390-cubic inch V-8s in 1967, the Camaro rolled out with 302-, 327-, 350- and 396-inch V-8s, with a choice of performance models. And the Camaro's styling was much smoother, less boxy, than the Mustang's.

The introduction of the Camaro threw ponycar development into a frenzy. Before the Camaro, the ponycar-class Mustang and Barracuda were not quite considered full musclecars by those who cared about such things. While average citizens snapped up six-cylinder and small-V-8 Mustangs, most serious performance enthusiasts still opted for intermediate-sized GTOs, Chevelle Super Sports, or monster-engined Mopar taxi cabs. But the Camaro (and Firebird) helped

change the street perception of the value of these 3/4-scale sport coupes. The race-ready Z28 and the stout SS-396 were clearly not just cute transportation. They were respected at traffic light drags, and the Camaro lured many intermediate owners its way. To compete, Ford had to resort to stuffing the Mustang full of 428 Cobra Jet, Boss 302, and Boss 429 engines. Plymouth opened up the Barracuda's mouth large enough to accept 440 and 426 Hemi V-8s. The 1970 Dodge Challenger followed the performance formula upon its introduction.

And while Ford may have had Carroll Shelby to create an exciting aura around the Mustang, the Camaro had nearly a half-dozen "Shelbys" of its own. Names like Yenko, Baldwin/Motion, Dana, Nickey, and Berger immediately helped the Camaro establish itself as

Has there ever been a more frequently modified American car than the Chevy Camaro? It's doubtful, as the Camaro has proved irresistible to hot rodders and racers alike. The combination of small-block Chevy V-8, compact size, and great looks has made the Camaro a natural canvas for automotive expression. Although many Camaros are restored to better-than-new condition today, in their prime most Camaros were quickly relieved of their factory hubcaps, smog controls, and air cleaners. Mag wheels, blowers, nitrous bottles, and performance bolt-ons usually took their place.

The Great War–Camaro versus Mustang

The Camaro's natural foe from Dearborn, the Mustang, has usually led the sales race between the two. The Mustang got the early start and, to its credit, hit the demographic target dead-center in 1964. But when the Mustang faltered, as in the late 1970s when it shared more with the Pinto than one of Shelby's Cobras, the Camaro roared ahead. And even in years where the Camaro lagged behind, the corporate combination of Camaro and Firebird sales often exceeded the Mustang's numbers.

As one looks at the sales data from more current times, though, it could also be argued that both cars have strayed a bit too far from their roots. Both cars were smaller, lighter, and cheaper upon their introduction than they are today, and even now the most loyal fans of both makes prefer the first-generation cars. The Mustang and Camaro were both entry-level cars people of all ages enjoyed; now they are altogether more serious. To be fair, much of that can be attributed to government safety and emission regulations, which add pounds and a pound's worth of dollars to the price of each new car. But a lot of it comes from trying to incorporate more features and luxuries than the original engineers ever dreamed of.

Good looks, a low price, and a powerful V-8 engine are the only real necessities in this market, and both Ford and Chevrolet have done better when they realized this. Listed are the Mustang and Camaro production figures through 1990:

	Camaro	Mustang
1965 (early)	–	121,538
1965	–	559,451
1966	–	607,568
1967	220,906	472,121
1968	235,147	317,404
1969	243,085	299,824
1970	124,901	190,727
1971	114,630	149,678
1972	68,651	125,093
1973	96,751	134,867
1974	151,008	385,993
1975	145,770	188,575
1976	182,959	187,567
1977	218,853	153,573
1978	272,631	192,410
1979	282,571	369,936
1980	152,005	271,322
1981	126,139	182,552
1982	189,747	130,418
1983	154,381	120,873
1984	261,591	141,480
1985	180,018	156,515
1986	192,219	224,410
1987	137,760	159,145
1988	96,275	211,225
1989	110,739	209,769
1990	34,986	128,179

the premier high-performance ponycar. Although Chevrolet never officially offered a 427 Camaro, these speed-minded establishments were all happy to create one, or order one clandestinely through fleet purchase channels.

Camaro sales increased each year from 1967 to 1969, proving Chevrolet had nailed the execution. To this day, the first-generation Camaros remain the favorite of enthusiasts. This was a hard act to follow, but somehow Chevrolet kept the momentum going with the introduction of the 1970 Camaro. When *that* car was introduced, it was like a futuristic show car come to life. The styling was of a type usually seen only on Italian exotics. Even better, it was a genuinely improved car. The basic body style was strong enough to last for 12 seasons.

The Camaro brings a bad-boy image to the street and the track. The car never strayed far from racing, even when Chevrolet was not officially involved. It is at home drag racing, road racing, and racing away from convenience stores after hold-ups. In mainstream media, the Camaro's image has

A dual four-barrel carburetor option, along with optional four-wheel disc brakes helped enshrine the 1969 Z28 as the top Camaro in many people's minds. The dual four-barrel option cost approximately $500 and was installed at the dealership rather than the factory. *Roger Huntington Collection/Dobbs Publishing Group*

When the Camaro was given a sultry new body in 1970, press accolades gushed forth as if the dam had burst at Lake Superlative. Chevrolet was widely lauded for creating a shape that would not be out of place in an Italian garage and for immediately making all other ponycars look clunky. The 1970's late introduction kept sales below 1969 levels, however. *Detroit Public Library National Automotive History Collection*

Chevrolet Camaros have paced the Indianapolis 500 four times—in 1967, 1969, 1982, and 1993. Each time the festival cars and replicas quickly became collectibles. The most numerous are the 1982 Pace Car Replicas; the rarest are the 1967 models. *Chevrolet*

been tied to drug dealers, bag men, lookouts, car thieves, and latter-day Bonnies and Clydes. The primered, jacked-up, stereoblasting Camaro has become a cliché in its own right—sometimes giving the car a reputation its creators would just as soon forget.

From a street-performance standpoint, the Camaro has come full circle during its three decades of life. Faster than most Mustangs upon its introduction and throughout the 1970s, the performance Camaros were generally slower than most Mustangs through the 1980s. The Camaro came into the world just as the Mustangs were starting to bulk up, and the portlier Mustangs were often victims of hard-charging Camaros. Twenty years later, the Ford had the advantage of lower weight, and a quick-revving, 5.0-liter small-block worked wonders in propelling the inexpensive Fox-chassis Mustang. However, after the 1993 model's introduction, the Camaro has definitely been back in front. The Camaro only has one V-8, but it's a slightly detuned Corvette engine, and that is more than Ford has been able to match in recent years.

Although not yet recognized by collectors or restorers, the most popular Camaros were those from the 1970s. After a decade of playing catch-up, Camaro sales finally surpassed the Mustang's in 1977, as the Mustang abdicated all attempts at performance. The Mustang II Cobra II may have been suitable for one of Charlie's Angels but hardly for anyone interested in recreational driving. The Z28, meanwhile, even in its weakest years was still one of the top performance cars in America.

Which other Camaros have been popular? Each of the 1967–1969 first-generation cars saw production of more than 220,000 cars per year. The peak year for Camaro production and sales was the 1979 model year when 282,571 were built, including 84,877 Z28s. The 1978 models were the next most popular Camaro. This late 1970s surge in sales coincided with a majority of baby-boomers reaching their 30-something years, when incomes are high and family responsibilities, if any, are few, especially for a generation known for postponing marriage.

Few cars live long enough to celebrate 30th anniversaries, but the Camaro has survived to secure the honor. Chevrolet commemorated the Camaro's 30th birthday with a special anniversary edition, featuring white paint covered by Hugger Orange stripes, a combination last seen on the 1969 Indy Pace Car. *Chevrolet*

The last great year, and the last with production above 200,000 units, was 1984. A buoyant economy, combined with a newly introduced 5.0 H.O. V-8, helped return the Camaro to glory days. The 100,899 Z28s built that year represent the highest number of Z28s ever built. The worst year, on paper, was 1990, with only 34,986 Camaros produced—although that was due to an early spring 1990 introduction of the 1991 Camaros, shortening the 1990 model year. Plus, the early 1990s recession didn't help matters. In reality, the worst year for the Camaro was 1972, when labor strife and a withering high-performance auto market nearly killed the Camaro for good.

Fortunately for car enthusiasts, and GM, the Camaro survived. Although there have been peaks and valleys, the Camaro's sales and image through the years have more than justified the corporation's investment. Despite the successes, there is a question about the Camaro's long-term survival. Demographics change, and the baby-boom bulge was followed by the smaller Generation-X, many of whom were raised on imported cars and thumping stereos instead of musclecars with thumping engines. Throughout most of the 1990s, Chevrolet has struggled to keep annual Camaro sales above 100,000, often failing—which must be frustrating to Chevrolet engineers and designers as the mid-1990s Camaros are arguably the best Camaros ever built.

As this is written, stone-stock new Z28s are capable of 13.8-second quarter-mile times. Handling, safety, and emissions have never been better. The SS option has even been revived. And best of all for Chevy fans, the Mustang again runs a distant second-place in the bang-for-the-buck wars. There has never been a better time to buy a Camaro. But then, each year—for more than 30 years—plenty of satisfied buyers have had the same thought.

The SS name was revived for the Camaro in 1996, to good effect. Shown is the 1998 Camaro SS, the most powerful Camaro since the days of big-block V-8s. *SLP Engineering*

Left
Besides pacing the Indianapolis 500 on four occasions, the Camaro was also selected as the pace car for the 1997 Brickyard 400 NASCAR race at Indy. The 1997 30th anniversary Brickyard Camaro was a dead-ringer for its 1969 Indy counterpart.

Brother in Arms—
The Firebird

The Mustang may have been the Camaro's chief opponent on the street, but the Camaro has also had a constant rival from within–Pontiac's Firebird. To the casual observer, the two cars battle each other for sales at the dealership and wins at the race track, much as other GM cars compete. But the rivalry is deeper than that. Since the two cars by necessity must share parts, each time a new F-body is in the design stages the Camaro and Firebird teams compete to express their vision of what the car should be. The Camaro team knows what fits in with Chevrolet's image and proposes their Camaro accordingly, and the Firebird team knows what suits Pontiac best and makes its case.

In the 1960s, both Pontiac and Chevrolet nearly got their wish for separate cars. Pontiac General Manager John Z. DeLorean had been agitating for a Pontiac-specific sports car for some time. The fiberglass XP-833 show car was DeLorean's idea for a suitable vehicle for the division, but since the two-seater would compete so directly with the Corvette, it was not given approval by the GM hierarchy. Pontiac was given instead a green light for its own version of the four-seat F-car. And so the 30-year internal rivalry began.

The first generation cars produced from 1967 to 1969 were definitely more the product of Chevrolet planning. Pontiac was not given the final go-ahead for the Firebird until late in the game, and by then Chevrolet had set the parameters for the car. Much of the car's mechanicals, such as the "Monoplate" single-leaf rear springs, were taken straight from the Chevrolet parts shelf. Chevrolet developed the earliest running prototypes and then handed one to Pontiac for development into a Firebird.

Due to the late decision, the Firebird debuted February 23, 1967, long after all the hoopla generated by the fall introduction of the 1967 new cars. Right up until the end, Pontiac was leaning toward naming the car the "Banshee," until they actually looked up Banshee in the dictionary and discovered the word, in Irish folklore, referred to a wailing spirit that appears before a family as a sign that one of them would soon die. Wisely figuring a spirit of death might not be the best sales pitch, Pontiac opted for "Firebird," a name used on several General Motors turbine-powered show cars.

The 1967 Firebird shared the Camaro's bodyshell, although it had the distinctive Pontiac nose and taillights, its own hood design, and some unique simulated vents on the rear quarter panels. The interior was nearly indistinguishable from the Camaro's. Chassis parts were shared, although each division could tune their respective car through selection of bushings and shock absorbers.

Pontiac built distinctly different engines than Chevrolet, which distinguished the Firebird from the Camaro under the hood. The Firebird offered a more international flavor, with an overhead cam six-cylinder engine at the bottom of the line-up. The Firebird came standard with a 230-cubic inch overhead-cam (OHC) six-cylinder, followed by a Sprint 230 OHC six, rated at 215 horsepower, 326 cubic inch V-8s in two- or four-barrel form, and a 400-inch V-8 rated at 325 horsepower. Prices started about $50 higher than comparable Camaros.

Although the engine line-up and Pontiac front end distinguished the Firebird, the sharing of parts was not lost on the press. "Because the Firebird shares the same body shell with the Camaro, the two resemble each other much more so–both in looks and feel–than do the Cougar and Mustang," noted Motor Trend in May 1967. But there were some improvements. "The Firebird isn't as prone to wheel hop and bottoming as some Camaros we've driven, and it has a tauter, more confidence-inspiring feel in all situations."

The Firebird really started to establish itself as a distinct car in 1969, with the introduction of the Trans-Am model. True, only 697 Pontiac Trans-Ams were produced in 1969 (although that's more than the number of Z28s Chevrolet produced in 1967), and ironically the Trans-Am never really was competitive in the SCCA Trans-Am racing series. But the Trans-Am, with its stripes, wings, and finely-tuned suspension, gave the Firebird a unique place in the musclecar universe. The Trans-Am is the only musclecar model continually in production since the 1960s and, as such, has become arguably the most recognized Pontiac of the era.

There was more Pontiac influence in the second-generation F-car introduced in 1970. Pontiac engineers and designers were involved from the beginning, and much of the F-car's looks comes from their efforts. The Trans-Am evolved into an even more distinctive car, with a backwards-facing hood scoop, an engine-turned aluminum dash, and large Firebird decals (sometimes derisively referred to as the "screaming chicken").

The glory years for the Firebird were clearly the 1970s. Pontiac's ponycar lived in the Camaro's shadow for most of its early years, but the car's popularity sprouted in the mid-1970s. As one of the only cars to offer real muscle underhood in that emissions-strangled decade, the Trans-Am's popularity skyrocketed. No Camaro ever carried 455 cubic inches underhood, and

The Firebird has been the Camaro's rival and corporate cousin since 1967. Shown is the line-up of 1994 Firebirds, including the Coupe, Formula, Trans-Am, and Trans-Am GT. *Pontiac*

even when that engine was retired, the 400-inch V-8 was more than was available elsewhere.

During most of the 1970s, the Camaro's main rival came not from Dearborn but from its competitor within the corporation. In 1977, Pontiac produced 68,744 Trans-Ams alone, followed by 93,341 be-winged 'Birds in 1978. In the 1979 model year Pontiac moved 117,109 Trans-Ams out the factory door, a higher total than in any year of Z28 production.

As General Motors' various cost-cutting policies in the 1980s and 1990s were implemented, the differences between the Camaro and Firebird have diminished. The last truly distinct Trans-Ams were the turbocharged 301-cubic inch V-8 models of 1980 and 1981 and the 3.8-liter turbocharged 25th anniversary cars of 1989. Since 1982 the Firebird Formula and Trans-Am have relied on the small-block Chevy V-8 for power, ending one of the major

ways the Camaro and Firebird were distinct. The corporate engine swapping has even been a two-way street, with Pontiac's 2.5-liter Iron Duke four-cylinder available in the Camaro starting in 1982.

Still, if the two cars are less unique than they once were, that doesn't mean they are worse. The Firebird has shared in the upward mobility of the Chevrolet V-8, and with the LT1 5.7 liter and now the LS1 V-8 with its 305 horsepower, the Pontiac Trans-Am has once again established itself at the front of the pack. The new car's styling is distinctly different than that of the Camaro, and the newer Firebirds have usually offered a better ride than the Camaro, giving buyers a nice alternative. As a sibling rivalry, the contest between the Camaro and Firebird can best be compared to two brothers playing football on the front yard. They'll knock heads for a while, but soon enough they'll be side by side, looking for two other kids to beat up on.

2

Chapter
Two

Panther Stalks Mustang:
1967-1968

Although the Camaro was a new car, few cars are truly new. The economics of car development dictate most new cars share a number of their components with other vehicles in a manufacturer's line. Most Chevrolets of the 1960s were all powered by one or another version of the famous small-block or big-block Chevy V-8 engines, and chassis components were shared whenever feasible. The Camaro was no exception. Although the car brought its own unique features to the market, such as the Z28's 302-cubic inch V-8, it also shared much with its corporate stablemate, the Chevy II.

Mechanically, the Camaro used a semi-unibody design that featured a unitized main body structure with a bolt-on front subframe that carried the engine and front suspension. Monoplate single-leaf rear springs, as introduced on the Chevy II, were also penciled in for the Camaro. The single-leaf spring design eliminated corrosion between leafs, which, in theory, contributed to longer spring life. And, of course, the Camaro's engines were right off the corporate parts shelves; even the new-for-1967 350 was not a truly new engine, just the latest update of the small-block V-8 introduced in 1955.

The engineering challenge was to combine economy car parts with the new pieces and turn them into a performance car. Fortunately, the Chevy team was up to the challenge and eager to create a car to dethrone the Mustang. Chuck Hughes (later Camaro chief engineer) was a development engineer at the time of the Camaro's creation. He headed part of the development activity at the Milford proving grounds and had previously worked at GM's noise and vibration facility. Hughes remembered when the Camaro first showed up at the proving grounds.

"Everyone was *really* enthused about it," he recalled. "And of course, at that time when the car came out, it was not as heavy a car, so you could get very good performance with very light powertrains, which is what you'd like to do. You'd like not to have behemoths out there. And so that was really a good time, before we were loaded down with so many, many, many government requirements," he said.

Much of the development team's focus ended up on the rear suspension. "They

All 1967 Indy Pace Cars were Super Sport/RS models, painted white with blue interiors. Approximately 100 were used at the track during the Indy 500's buildup; they were then sold as used cars.

The L78, 375-horsepower, 396-cubic inch V-8 was ordered in only 1,138 1967 Camaros, and perhaps only a handful of the 100 or so Pace Car Replicas were equipped with this top-of-the-line engine. The L78 was a $500.30 option and teamed only with the Super Sport package.

With a trunk that was barely larger than the glovebox of full-size GM sedans, the Camaro and Firebird had to improvise to find additional room. In 1968, a space-saver spare became available, one of the earliest on an American car.

[the Camaros] were not without problems when they came," Hughes said. He remembers three prototype test cars that cost about $500,000 each. His group spent some time with the vehicles and recommended things that should be changed before production. But because of the expense involved with building prototype cars, Hughes said, "you don't do some of the abusive things that you ought to do." That attitude changed after one of the prototypes was sent to Pontiac because that division was developing the Firebird.

Hughes recalled: "The Pontiac development engineers called up and said, 'Hey, what are you doing about power hop?' And we said, 'What do you mean, power hop? We haven't seen the problem.' And then they described how to get it. Then, Christ, we were getting it all over the place.

"We were all pretty enthused about [the Camaro project] until we discovered the power hop. When it really sets off, it goes through quite large deflections. There was considerable analysis with high-speed

Convertible Camaros offered better headroom than the coupe models, although dramatically reduced rear-seat hip and shoulder room, as back-seat passengers paid the price for the room required to stow the top. The convertible also weighed 200 to 300 pounds more than a comparable coupe. The owner of this 1967 Pace Car has equipped his car with flag brackets, as might have been done in the car's youth.

All 1967 Indy Pace Cars came with the blue Custom Interiors. The walnut-grained steering wheel was a $31 option. The few cars equipped with the 375-horsepower 396 were fitted with tachometers that red lined at 6,000 rpm, while lesser engines showed a 5,500-rpm red line.

movies and lot of people with their heads together." According to Hughes, the consensus opinion was to combat the power hop by staggering the shocks. "That required major body retooling," Hughes said.

Although the Monoplate rear springs are often singled out as the culprit, Hughes recalls, "It didn't make any difference whether we had multi-leaf springs or not. It had to do with the pitch mode of the axle winding up. It was a fairly soft mode, winding up the springs, and stiffness was about the same whether [the springs were] mono-leaf or multi-leaf."

As it turned out, the wheel hop was the chief complaint about the Camaro upon its introduction. Chevrolet developed a short-term fix to the wheel hop problem with a right-side traction bar for the 1967 Z28 and some of the other V-8 four-speed Camaros introduced later in the model year. The true fix would not come until 1968.

The 1967 Firebird shared many of the Camaro's strengths and weaknesses. It used much of the same hardware under the skin, although Pontiac engineers used their own

One of the early Camaro's handicaps was a convoluted, restrictive exhaust system. All Camaros rode on single-leaf "Monoplate" rear springs in 1967. A right-side traction bar on high-performance models that year helped control wheel hop.

William "Bill" Mitchell stands beside the new 1967 Camaro. Mitchell was General Motors vice president of design during the Camaro's conception. Mitchell was known for his love of sports cars and clean automotive styling, which was revealed in the 1965 Corvair's bodywork. He was also known to drive his subordinates hard. Mitchell kept the design standards high by guiding the styling of the Camaro's 1970 re-do. *Detroit Public Library National Automotive History Collection*

mass of the vehicle was. Then we made fully enclosed containers with steel springs and fluid in those. So the initial ones were done on that convertible."

When the Camaro came around, it presented the same problem. "And then the design engineers and Fisher Body started understanding what we were doing. So when it came time for the Camaro convertible, we were watching for that," Hughes said. "And they said, 'Yep, we're going to need them.' So they just planned the space for them and everything. It was not an afterthought, we'd already had the experience."

The Camaro also incorporated leading-edge safety features such as a dual-circuit master cylinder and a collapsible steering column. Power front disc brakes were optional.

On Display

After a two-year gestation period, the Camaro's official public introduction came from Chevrolet General Manager Pete Estes on September 12, 1966, at the GM proving grounds. The Camaro arrived in four different versions: six-cylinder Sport Coupe, six-cylinder convertible, V-8 Sport Coupe, and V-8 convertible. Engines choices began with the 230-cubic inch six-cylinder and went up the ladder to the 250-inch six-cylinder, 327-cubic inch V-8 with either two- or four-barrel carburetor, and the 350-cubic inch, four-barrel V-8, which was a Camaro exclusive.

The Camaro was 184.6 inches long, slightly longer than the Mustang but shorter than Plymouth's Barracuda. Chevrolet was the only one of the manufacturers to not offer a fastback in this class. The Camaro stretched 72.5 inches in width, which was the widest of the three major ponycars. The Camaro had the widest track, which contributed to its handling abilities. As for weight, the Camaro slotted between the lighter Mustang and heavier Barracuda. The Camaro gas tank held 18.5 gallons of fuel.

The least expensive Camaro was the six-cylinder Sport Coupe, which started at $2,466. The V-8 model started at $2,572 and came with the 210-horsepower, two-barrel 327. Upgrading to the four-barrel, 275-horsepower 327 cost $92. A three-speed manual transmission was standard for all models, with a four-speed manual and the two-speed Powerglide automatic optional.

The Camaro also boasted the first application of the most famous of all small-block Chevy V-8s, the 350. Available only with the performance-oriented SS package, the 350 was rated at 295 horsepower. Taking the

suspension settings to impart a slightly different "feel" to the driver. Additionally, the Firebird was distinguished by its own engine line-up: two versions of Pontiac's overhead-cam, six-cylinder, a two- and four-barrel 326-cubic inch V-8, and a 325-horsepower, 400-cubic inch V-8. Nonetheless, the Firebird was also hobbled by power hop problems resulting from the rear suspension package.

Another source of concern during Camaro development was torsional vibration in the convertible models. Removing the roof panel—a major structural component on a unibody car—contributed to body flex and vibration. But Chevrolet had faced this problem before. The solution involved placing large tuned vibration dampers in each corner, an idea first applied on the Corvair convertible. These dampers canceled out the torsional vibrations.

Hughes recalled the origin of the unique dampers. "I did those first on the Corvair. I'll never forget as long as I live," he recalled. "I was a supervisor but a fairly new supervisor. All the people in the place knew I knew how to solve problems. My boss said, 'I want to see if you can go save this car [the Corvair].' It was just too weak in torsion. In about three or four days I had a facsimile of tuned absorbers in the corners. My training and background was vibration, so I knew what to do. So initially I had rubber springs and lead weights for the tuned mass. That allowed me to optimize how much mass I needed because I didn't know what the equivalent

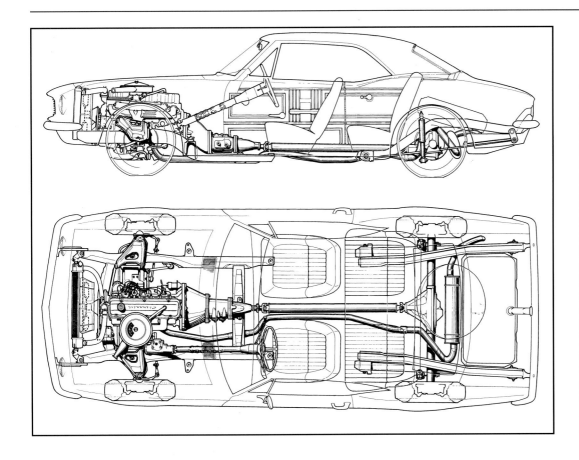

This cutaway illustration reveals the 1967 Camaro's strengths and weaknesses. The semi-unit body consisted of a front subframe that bolted to the main unit body with four large, rubber insulated bolts. In the debit column are the upright shocks mounted in front of the axle that allowed axle tramp under hard acceleration and the restrictive muffler arrangement. Shown is the base model 230-cubic inch six, with three-speed manual transmission, column-mounted shifter, and four-wheel drum brakes. *Roger Huntington Collection/Dobbs Publishing Group*

The 1967 SS-350 was the first high-performance Camaro available to the public. The 350-cubic inch V-8, a Camaro exclusive in 1967, was only available with the SS equipment that year. Cutaway reveals the single-leaf rear springs used on all models in 1967 and details of the semi-unitized construction. *Detroit Public Library National Automotive History Collection*

Following pages
The most economical Camaro available in 1967 was the six-cylinder Sport Coupe, with a base price of $2,466. The RPO Z21 special trim group dressed up the Camaro with wheel-opening moldings and drip-rail moldings. The owners of this car have equipped their Camaro with optional Rally wheels.

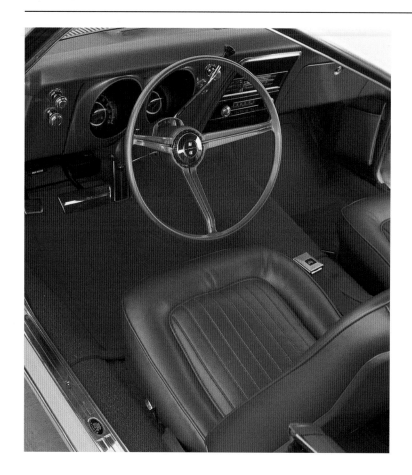

small-block V-8 to 350 cubic inches involved keeping the 327's 4.0-inch bore but increasing the stroke to 3.48 inches. The 350's crankshaft journal diameter was increased to improve strength. The engineers' work was worth the effort, as the 350 offered the best compromise between large displacement and light weight. At the proving ground, development engineer Hughes was immediately impressed. "It was like driving a DC [electric] motor," he said. "The torque comes up and just stays there, never mind rpm."

The 350 V-8 was teamed with the SS option to present a worthy performance package. The SS option included special heavy-duty suspension, a "bumblebee" stripe around the nose, a domed hood with simulated vents, SS identification on the fenders, an SS gas cap, a unique grille with an SS-350 emblem, an SS steering wheel, and D70x14 red-stripe tires. Chevrolet played up the striped visage with a "Meet the masked marvel" ad campaign.

The major appearance package for the Camaro was the Rally Sport option. For $105 it included electrically-operated headlamp doors, parking lamps relocated to the front valance, lower bodyside moldings, back-up lamps relocated below the rear bumper,

Although entry-level Camaros were often stripped-down affairs, Chevrolet's build-your-own-option philosophy allowed for several ways to brighten the otherwise plain exteriors and vinyl interiors. This car is equipped with RPO Z21 special trim group and Z23 special interior group. The Z23 special interior group included such items as the bright trim on the pedal pads. The 1967's dash was unique to that year, with padding only on the top.

The base Camaro engine in 1967 was the 140-horsepower 230-cubic inch six-cylinder. The 155-horsepower, 250-cubic inch six, shown here, was a $26 option. The 230 was only available in first-generation Camaros; in 1970, the 250 became the base engine.

wheel-opening moldings, drip-rail moldings, black taillamp bezels, and RS emblems on the grille, gas cap, and fenders. If the RS option was ordered on a Super Sport, the SS badges were used.

An eager press corps wasted no time flogging the Camaro and reporting the results. *Popular Mechanics* (October 1966) summed up the conclusions of many: "Tabbed since its inception the 'F-Car' by GM and the 'Panther' by everybody else—including the competition—it's the car Chevy rushed to production when it became painfully apparent even heated-up versions of the Corvair were no match for Ford's front-running Mustang. But there's nothing 'rushed' about the final product; it's a tidy, handsome, and spirited little car that should warm the hearts of all Chevy enthusiasts."

Hot Rod magazine concurred in its November 1966 appraisal: "Indications stemming from a pre-introductory drive-test give promise of a very road-worthy automobile that should give the horse a good run for the money." Reviewers in general were favorable but also noted the car's shortcomings. Like most ponycars, the Camaro's trunk was about the size of a post-office box, but at least there was an optional folding rear seatback that helped open the space somewhat. Another common criticism was the poor location of the optional "Special Instruments Package" that placed the gauges far away on the floor.

Most of the attention, though, was focused on the hot rod of the bunch, the SS-350. *Car Life* tested a 1967 SS-350 and recorded a quarter-mile elapsed time of 15.8 seconds at 89 miles per hour. Of the car's handling, they noted, "The Camaro corners in a relatively flat attitude, without that annoying front-end tucking that is so apparent in other cars. The feeling, despite a quick but quite insensitive power steering, is that the car is inordinately nimble."

Motor Trend editors also tested an SS-350 in December 1966 with slightly better results. Their quarter-mile drag test showed 15.4 seconds at 90 miles per hour. "Our SS-350 test car really surprised us," they confessed. "Quarter-mile times were exceptionally good, especially considering the over-3,500-pound weight, with two passengers plus test equipment aboard. We've tested some comparably equipped cars that were considerably slower." Later, in their May 1967 issue, they compared the Camaro to its logical competitors, the Mustang and Barracuda. While generally praising the Camaro,

When both SS and RS equipment was ordered, the SS emblems and stripes took precedence. The main external clue to the RS presence were the hidden headlamps. Although a sport model, the SS came standard with hubcaps; Rally wheels were optional. A vinyl top was a $73 option.

they found more to criticize the second time around. "There's a dearth of instruments on the Camaro as standard equipment," they wrote. "If you want others they cost extra and go down by the console. But if you also want the optional stereo tape, you're out of luck. Since they occupy the same spot, you can have one or the other, but not both."

It was when banging around on the SS-350 that most of the magazines discovered the wheel hop that had so haunted the engineers during development. As *Hot Rod* noted, "We'll underwrite the fact that those single-leaf springs are not the dragman's dream, but Chevy's gone and put a neat traction bar on the right rear, curing much of the wheel hop." With fresh spark plugs and a recurved ignition, *Hot Rod* editors cemented their reputations as dragmasters by clocking a 14.85 at 95.65 miles per hour out of their test SS-350, and a 15.05 before the tune.

The 350 was the top engine for exactly two months until the 396 big-block was slipped into the Camaro line-up in November. With the Barracuda offering a 383-cubic inch V-8, the Mustang a 390, and Pontiac's Firebird a 400, it was inevitable that

The only sure external clues to the 1967 Z28's nature were the twin racing stripes atop the hood and trunk lid. The Z28's designation came from the "Special Performance Package's" option code and was not originally given special Z28 emblems or trim. Rally wheels were part of the package though, along with all the serious under-the-skin hardware. Total Z28 production in 1967 was 602 cars.
Mike Mueller

Chevrolet would follow suit. As with the 350, ordering either the 325-horsepower L35 or the 375-horsepower L78 396 engine netted the buyer the SS gear.

Whereas the L35 was basically a full-size passenger car V-8, the L78 was built strictly for performance. Its 375 horsepower came courtesy of 2.19-inch intake valves (compared to 2.06-inch on the L35), an aluminum intake manifold topped by a huge, thirsty carburetor, and header-type exhaust manifolds. The block had four-bolt mains, and the blocks were drilled and tapped for oil cooler lines.

Stuffing a big-car engine in the trim Camaro made for impressive acceleration but also changed the character of the car thanks to the extra weight over the front wheels. At the proving grounds, Chuck Hughes recalled that the 396 was not to his tastes. "That was not one of my favorite programs because it took a fairly agile car and made a truck out

of it," he said. "By the time you put the 396 in there, it was a go-fast, go-straight torquey car, but not fun to drive. And we had to do a lot of things like move the power-steering pump pressure up to be able to do curb push-away," he said. It also required extra tire and brake development to accommodate the heavier mass.

Getting Serious

In addition to the SS-350 and SS-396, there was a third distinct performance Camaro launched in 1967, the legendary Z28. Given General Motors' corporate policies and politics of the time, it seems a miracle that such a single-minded car emerged from the company. After all, Chevy was officially out of racing and had been for a decade. In the 1960s GM was still abiding by the Automobile Manufacturers Association's (AMA) 1957 ban on factory-supported racing. Few large corporations want to be labeled irresponsible, and

the AMA had long since made its case that factory-sponsored racing gave the appearance of sanctioning reckless driving behavior.

Ford abided by the ban for a while, too, before wadding up the agreement and tossing it down a four-barrel carburetor in the early 1960s. Ford then used racing to great advantage in the early part of the decade, winning the Indianapolis 500 in 1965 in Jim Clark's Ford-powered Lotus and 48 of 55 NASCAR Grand National races that year, after bagging 30 wins the year before. In sports car racing, Shelby's Cobras were smacking around the privateer Corvettes. Chrysler was also much more aggressive in NASCAR, and especially in drag racing.

Chevrolet was faced with the dilemma of obeying GM's acceptance of the AMA ban on racing, while simultaneously selling a sporty car to the youth market—and the youth market didn't like losers. Chevrolet's solution involved much winking and nudging and clandestine activity, while producing assorted "heavy-duty" parts that could be sold to private racers, without actually giving money to racing teams or advertising victories.

In the Camaro's case, the perfect venue for racing was the Sports Car Club of America's (SCCA) new Trans-Am Sedan Championship series. The Trans-Am followed international Group II sedan rules, while offering a coveted prize—a manufacturers' championship that promised considerable bragging

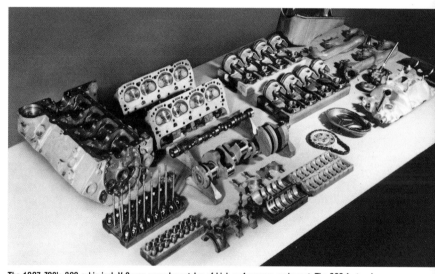

The 1967 Z28's 302-cubic inch V-8 was a regular catalog of high-performance equipment. The 302 featured a forged crankshaft, forged pistons, a windage tray, a solid-lifter cam, large 2.02-inch intake valves and 1.60-inch exhaust valves, an aluminum intake manifold, a 780-cubic feet per minute Holley four-barrel, a special cooling system, and a special exhaust. The factory rating of 290 horsepower was widely considered to be a serious case of sandbagging by GM. *Roger Huntington Collection/Dobbs Publishing Group*

rights. Two manufacturers' championships were offered: over-2-liter cars and under-2-liter cars. The first race was run on March 25, 1966, perfect timing for the ponycar boom. Mustangs were a factor immediately, and the over-2-liter class in the Trans-Am series was clearly the natural home for ponycars of all stripes.

Dick Harrell was one of the top Camaro drivers in drag racing, piloting both the Yenko Super Camaro Dealers Funny Car and later a Fred Gibb ZL1 427 Camaro. *Greg Rager collection*

Dick Harrell (left) accepts congratulations from Don Yenko after a victory in the Yenko Funny Car Camaro. Don Yenko was used to being congratulated after victories himself, having established a successful racing career before establishing himself as one of the most prominent car dealers in racing. *Courtesy Greg Rager collection*

One obstacle to overcome, though, was the Trans-Am series' 305-cubic inch engine displacement limit. Chevrolet had already decided the Camaro's smallest production V-8 would be the 327, too large for T/A competition. Chevy still manufactured the 283, but it was not known as a performance beast and would give up 20 cubic inches to the competition. Something new had to be created, something that could pass the SCCA's homologation requirements and win on the track.

Vince Piggins, then Chevrolet product promotion manager, was instrumental in the Z28's creation. The idea was to produce a Camaro that, if not actually officially raced by Chevrolet, would come with all the good stuff so capable racing teams could realistically win in Trans-Am. And racing teams didn't come much more capable than Roger Penske's, who showed up on Chevy's doorstep wanting to be the first to race the new Camaro. Penske also had a willing sponsor, the Sun Oil Company.

Piggins' team had worked up a street/race prototype that was displayed at Riverside in late November. It went into production December 29, known as the Z28. The Z28 got its name from its position on the list of factory-option packages. For example, regular production option (RPO) Z23 was a "special interior" package. RPO Z28 was the "Special Performance Package," but it also made a good name for the car.

The Z28 was both a handling package and a special engine package. The Z28 had exclusive use of the new 302 engine, rated at 290 horsepower at 5,800 rpm. Its displacement came from mating the 327 block with the 283 crankshaft, delivering a 4-inch bore and 3-inch stroke. In keeping with its race track nature, the 302 ran an 11.0:1 compression ratio with Chevrolet/TRW pistons, used a high-rise aluminum intake manifold, 800-cubic feet per minute Holley carburetor, a 0.485-inch lift solid-lifter cam, a forged crankshaft, forged-steel connecting rods, a windage tray, 5/16-inch pushrods, and large 2.02-inch intake valves, with 1.60-inch valves for the exhaust. Performance could be further enhanced by the optional plenum air intake, air cleaner, and headers. As with the 375-horsepower 396, air conditioning was not available with the 302.

The Z28 received special suspension tuning, 15x6-inch Rally wheels with 7.35x15 Red Stripe tires, quick-ratio steering, and a heavy-duty radiator. Checking the Z28 box required ordering power front-disc brakes and the close-ratio four-speed transmission. The standard axle ratio was 3.73:1.

Although no special nameplate graced the Z28's flanks, early Z28s were quickly identified by the twin rally stripes running over the hood and deck lid. The Z28 could be teamed with the Rally Sport option, though, giving the car hide-away headlamps. The Z28 was an impressive package on paper and in real life, although not terribly streetable, as most of the horsepower was generated high in the rpm range. The Z28 option cost $358 in 1967.

With the right driver, the Z28 could humiliate some much brawnier machinery. As *Motor Trend* noted in its May 1967 ponycar free-for-all, "The Z28 Camaro (four-speed standard) submitted for our test was behind at the 0–60 time compared to a 396 automatic but screamed ahead to win by a half-second and 5 miles per hour at the quarter-mile marker." Their Z28's ET was a respectable 14.8 at a high 96 miles per hour, compared to the 396 automatic's 15.4 at 92 miles per hour. Only the 396 four-speed was quicker, at 14.5 at 95 miles per hour.

On the track the car's peakiness and high-strung state of tune was a blessing, one

that quickly bore fruit. Penske's primary driver for the Trans-Am was rising star Mark Donohue. The clean-cut Donohue had an engineering background and brought a careful and deliberate style to the track. While fast, he rarely did stupid things and developed a huge following at the races. During the 1967 Trans-Am season, Mark Donohue won three races at Marlboro (with co-driver Craig Fisher), Stardust, and Seattle. There was a break-in period early while the Camaro racers figured out the car's strengths and weaknesses, but after Chevy engineers worked up heavy-duty spindles, axles, and other assorted parts, the Camaro was much tougher. It was a promising start, but Jerry Titus won the title for Ford in a Mustang.

An even more flagrant association with auto racing debuted in May. The Camaro was chosen as the 1967 Indianapolis 500 Pace Car, a major plum for any manufacturer. Besides the on-track cars, Chevrolet built approximately 100 parade and festival cars for use during the month-long build-up to the race. All were SS/RS convertibles, painted white with blue nose stripes and blue interiors. As Super Sports, they were powered by either 350 or 396 V-8s. The cars were easy to spot with their blue "Chevrolet Camaro Official Pace Car 51st Annual Indianapolis 500 Mile Race, May 30, 1967" lettering on the

From the factory, this Nickey 427 Camaro SS was equipped with an L78, 375-horsepower 396. After Nickey's surgery, the car emerged with a 435-horsepower, triple-two-barrel L71 Corvette 427 underhood. Buyers could order even more radical powerplants; the only limiting factor was money. *Mike Mueller*

Following pages
Nickey 427 Camaros were produced in cooperation with Bill Thomas Race Cars in California. The original owner of this Marina Blue car, who still owns it today, selected a number of dealer-installed performance items, including four-wheel metallic disc brakes, traction bars, a deep-tone exhaust, safety bell housing, safety block plates, and a heavy-duty dual-plate clutch. *Mike Mueller*

Camaro versus Mustang, 1967

The Camaro and Mustang were natural foes from birth, with owners (and corporations) glaring at each other through their respective ponycar windshields, revving engines, and hurling challenges. Starting in 1967, Camaro versus Mustang has become one of the best and longest-lived of automotive rivalries.

While the Camaro was all-new, the Mustang was given its first freshening for 1967. The Mustang grew for that year, with its larger body opening up room for Ford's 390-cubic inch big-block V-8. Carroll Shelby wasted no time in finding the next bigger engine, the 428 Police Interceptor, and dropping it in the Mustang to create the GT-500.

Mustang outsold Camaro in 1967, 472,121 to 220,906. Still, Chevrolet offered more engine options for the Camaro, with more horsepower throughout the range.

	Camaro	Mustang
Wheelbase (in)	108.1	108.0
Length (in)	184.6	183.6
Height (in)	51.0	51.8
Width (in)	72.5	70.9
Shpg. weight	2,770 lbs	2,578 lbs
Base price	$2,466	$2,461
Perf. option	SS pkg. $210	GT pkg. $205
	Z28 pkg. $358	
Engines	230-ci 6 cyl.	200-ci 6 cyl.
	250-ci 6 cyl.	289-ci V-8 (2 bbl)
	302-ci V-8 (4 bbl)	289-ci V-8 (4 bbl)
	327-ci V-8 (2 bbl)	289-ci V-8 (hi-pf)
	327-ci V-8 (4 bbl)	390-ci V-8 (4 bbl)
	350-ci V-8 (4 bbl)	
	396-ci V-8 (L35)	
	396-ci V-8 (L78)	

The Z28's 302 V-8 was dressed up with chrome valve covers and a chrome open-element air cleaner. Even the Z28 was not immune from air pollution regulations and wore an AIR pump for 1968. Being primarily a racing engine, air conditioning was not available with the 302-cubic inch V-8. *Roger Huntington Collection/ Dobbs Publishing Group*

doors. Mauri Rose, who won the race in 1941, 1947, and 1948, drove the actual Pace Car. A. J. Foyt, who would later pilot Camaros in the IROC series, won the race.

Excess, plus Some

Almost as soon as the first Camaro rolled out of the factory, performance-minded dealerships and maverick hot rodders started playing with this new toy from Chevrolet. Their first impulse, naturally enough, was more power, which was readily available

thanks to the largest V-8 Chevy offered, the mighty 427-cubic inch V-8. The L72 427 had been introduced in the Corvette in 1966, offering 425 horsepower and 460 pounds-feet of torque. For 1967, the 427 was sold in even more potent versions, one with 435 horsepower and triple-two-barrel carburetion. As the 427 was from the same engine family as the 396, the two did not differ in size externally, making engine swaps easy. Dropping a 427 in a Camaro guaranteed pee-your-pants acceleration and made the car an animal on the street or strip.

Several dealers that specialized in high-performance quickly figured this out. Among the most prominent was Yenko Chevrolet in Cannonsburg, Pennsylvania. Don Yenko had successfully raced Corvettes and other Chevrolets in the early 1960s and had considerable credibility within the high-performance world. He first started selling his own modified cars late in 1965, beginning with "Stinger" Corvairs. The Stinger was mostly designed with SCCA road racing in mind, so the cars came with a tightened suspension, the rear seats removed, exhaust modifications, a revised induction system, and steeper gearing.

Yenko started transplanting L72 427s in Camaros shortly after the car's introduction. For 1969, Yenko figured out a way to wrangle 427 Camaros out of the factory (see chapter 3), but in 1967 and 1968 the 427 Camaros were engine-swap cars. (Reportedly, a couple of Yenko's 1968 427 Camaros were actually built at Chevrolet as COPOs.)

There are few major external differences between the 1967 Camaros and the 1968 models, but there are a couple of visual clues. For 1968, the Camaro's vent windows were retired, and rectangular parking lamps replaced the round units used in 1967. The grille was also given more of a V-shape, compared to the flat grille of 1967. The front "bumblebee" stripe and rear-deck spoiler were available on any Camaro as RPO D91 for $14.75 and RPO D80 for $32.65. Convertible output was 20,440 cars in 1968, less than 10 percent of total Camaro production.

The 1967 Yenko Camaros were original-ly SS-350 cars, with the 427s swapped in. In 1968 Yenko started with SS-396 Camaros as a base, and swapped in the 427 short block while keeping the 396 heads and induction system. Yenko's efforts were set apart from other engine swappers because he started his own dealership network—people from all over the country could buy his cars. There were 54 427 Yenko Camaros built in 1967 and 64 more in 1968.

Also a pioneer in mining 427 Camaro gold was Dana Chevrolet, a South Gate, California, dealer. With Peyton Cramer (who had been instrumental in getting the Shelby

Mustang operation off the ground) as a new partner, Dana moved quickly to get the deal-er's performance projects up to speed. Rac-ers Don McCain and Dick Guldstrand were responsible for making Dana's 427 Camaro work. They started with SS-350 Camaros and swapped in the 425-horsepower Corvette L72 427s. The Dana 427 Camaros came with headers, as well as a heavy-duty clutch and pressure plate. And the option list was extensive. Buyers could opt for the Corvette's L71, triple-two-barrel 427, rated at 435 horsepower ($150 extra), or go for such attention-getters as a unique twin-scoop, functional fiberglass hood.

A column shift was standard equipment when the automatic transmission was ordered, as the floor shifter and console were optional. Custom Interior options included woodgrain trim on the instrument panel, special seat upholstery, and a passenger-side dash grab handle.

Car Life tested a Dana 427 Camaro and was awed by its power. "And some people think they have problems keeping the 350 Camaro at low altitude. They haven't seen anything. The 427 Camaro is just *too* much—in more ways than one," they wrote. They recorded a traction-limited 14.2-second quarter-mile at 102 miles per hour but knew that didn't show the car's true potential. "Chassis modifications and suitable tires should easily knock a full 2 seconds off the car's 14.2-second ET in the quarter-mile," they estimated. "Even without chassis tuning, the 427 Camaro will keep pace with just about anything operating on the streets of America today."

Another maker of monster Camaros was Berger Chevrolet in Grand Rapids, Michigan,

a dealer that was especially active in 1969 selling COPO 427 Camaros. Nickey Chevrolet in Chicago, known for the backwards "K" in the company's logo, was also very performance oriented, sponsoring many racers in a variety of motorsports arenas. To create their 427 Camaro, they teamed with Bill Thomas Race Cars in Anaheim, California. Thomas was well-connected in the performance world and offered West Coast facilities suitable for building the vehicles. "Nickey Camaro is the car that comes to you ready to race . . . ready to win right off the showroom floor," Nickey brochures promised. Ads emphasized service. "But, you get much more than parts at Nickey/Bill Thomas. We'll give you the know-how to make you GO and the know-how is yours FREE. There's never a charge for technical information."

Car and Driver tested a dual four-barrel, 550-horsepower 427 Nickey/Thomas Camaro in 1967. "The Nickey 427 Camaro is, no doubt about it, an attention-getter. It looks exactly like what it is—a Camaro with Mr. America musculature," they noted. "It is a very good attempt at making a dual-purpose vehicle for the Sunday sportsman, though all such creations must, of course, ultimately be a compromise." In performance testing, they recorded a 13.9-second quarter-mile at 108 miles per hour. A 13.9 was a relatively weak time for that much Camaro, but a serious lack of traction, the wide-ratio four-speed, and restrictive street mufflers were cited as reasons for the relatively slow time.

One of the wildest of the Camaro converters was Motion Performance in New York. They teamed with Baldwin Chevrolet to form the Baldwin/Motion alliance and hitched their wagon to the 427 engine swap. As with most of the other dealers, Motion Performance had an impressive hot rodding resume. Joel Rosen started his Motion speed shop in Brooklyn in 1958 and moved to Long Island in 1966. "We approached Baldwin Chevrolet with a program back in '67, and surprisingly, they went for it," Rosen recalled. Unlike Yenko, Baldwin/Motion did not set up a dealer network, and all cars were delivered through Baldwin Chevrolet or Motion Performance.

The Camaro was Baldwin/Motion's first project. "SS-427 Camaro is what's happening!" Motion's ads bragged. "Dyno-tuned and ready to wail . . . $3,650." Motion identified the Camaro's weaknesses early and addressed them with their "Super-Bite" suspension kits, which included custom-valved shocks, front- coil-spring risers, and bolt-on

Looking Good– Rally Sport Equipment

The Rally Sport option, although often teamed with Super Sport and Z28 equipment, was, in actuality, only an appearance package. While not contributing to actual performance, the Rally Sport option, with its hide-away headlamps and bold stripes, did much to enhance the Camaro's image. The $105.35 Rally Sport option (RPO Z22) offered essentially the same equipment in 1967 and 1968, although 1968 models switched from electric- to vacuum-operated headlamp doors. In 1967, 64,842 buyers selected the option; 40,977 followed in 1968.

Rally Sport Equipment, 1967
• Electrically-operated headlamp doors
• Lower body moldings
• Bodyside paint stripes
• Special grille
• RS emblems on grille, gas cap, and fenders
• Valance-mounted parking lamps
• Wheel-opening and drip-rail moldings
• Black painted taillamp bezels
• Special rear back-up lamps

The optional clock's lonely location was the transmission tunnel, at least if no floor console was ordered. The electric clock was a $15 option.

traction bars. "These bars are standard equipment on the SS-427 Motion Camaro and are guaranteed to stop axle and spring windup and wheel hop regardless of tires and engine output," ads promised.

Standard equipment for the Baldwin/Motion SS-427 Camaro included the 425-horsepower 427 V-8, Muncie four-speed close-ratio transmission, Positraction rear end with choice of gear ratio, the above-mentioned traction bars and sportier suspension, D70x14 Wide Oval red stripe tires, dual exhaust, SS-427 emblems and front accent band, chrome valve covers and air cleaner, modified ignition, heavy-duty radiator, and dyno tuning.

Baldwin/Motion's ultimate Camaro was the Phase III SS-427 Camaro, which was guaranteed to run 11-second quarter miles. It was upgraded with a huge Holley three-barrel carb, hotter cam, special ignition, and a host of other tuning tricks. Baldwin/Motion even offered a warranty on the cars, to a point. According to Baldwin Auto Company sales documents, the SS-427 warranty ran for 90 days or 4,000 miles—with some exceptions. "The L88 option, while available at an extra cost of $700 must be blueprinted at a cost of $500 additional," they specified.

"We do not recommend the L88 option for street use, and it does not carry a warranty."

The 427 bug was catching. "In '68, we expanded the line to include the rest of them, which were called the 'Fantastic Five,'" Rosen said. Everything Baldwin/Motion built was a swap, built to order, with their own long list of options. "We delivered anything," Rosen recalled and made no secret of the fact they were building street racers. "Our market was street cars, but, if you will, ultimate street cars, because you could buy whatever you wanted," he said. "We had a money-back guarantee that the cars would run in the 11s . . . and never had to make a refund," he added.

The cars were not just hype. *Cars* magazine labeled the 1967 L88 aluminum-head SS-427 Camaro they tested the "1967 top street eliminator." They cut an 11.50 quarter-mile at 125 miles per hour running on Prowler cheater slicks. "In three weeks of street testing we didn't come across a stock or modified street car that even came close to our Camaro's performance," they wrote.

Rodder & Super Stock magazine tested a 1968 Phase III L88 427 Baldwin/Motion SS-427 Camaro and came away with shaky knees. "Our first ride in the car scared the

Performance parts manufacturer Edelbrock used a 1968 Camaro SS as a rolling laboratory for intake manifold development. In particular, the 1968 was used in the development of big-block, race-only, tunnel-ram manifolds, including the TR-2X. During testing of the TR-2X on a 427 V-8, more than 600 horsepower was hiding (not very well) under the hood. *Roger Huntington Collection/Dobbs Publishing Group*

shorts off us," they admitted. "But once we got used to the fantastic sheer brute strength of it and treated it with respect, the car was easier to live with." How much brute strength? They recorded 12.00 at 114.50 miles per hour on street tires and an 11.48 with slicks and open exhaust.

1968

After a successful debut year with more than 200,000 Camaros sold, 1968 was a year of refinement and evolutionary change. External differences were subtle. The side vent windows were eliminated on both Camaro and Firebird as "Astro Ventilation" made its debut. Per government mandate, side marker lamps were incorporated on the fenders. Rectangular turn signal lamps in the grille replaced the round lamps used in 1967. The famous houndstooth cloth upholstery joined the option list.

The biggest functional change came from the introduction of staggered rear shocks, with one shock mounted ahead of the front axle, one behind. This reduced the power-hop problems Camaros and Firebirds had become famous for. Although the Monoplate, single-leaf rear springs remained in place on the lower-end models, performance Camaros were fitted with multi-leaf rear springs. One technically interesting bit of hardware for the 1968 Camaro was the Torque Drive transmission, which was available on six-cylinder cars. This semi-automatic offered manual shifting without a clutch, giving two forward speeds and one reverse.

Motor Trend was impressed with the transmission, with a few caveats. "The closest thing it can be compared with is the Powerglide because it is one—suddenly it's 1950," tester Eric Dahlquist wrote. "A cutaway drawing of the T-D shows it is indeed the familiar two-speed automatic with the automatic valve body, governor, vacuum modulator, high-speed downshift mechanism, and other trifles deleted. The whole deal is very clever, but it begs the question: Why, since it is very similar to a regular automatic, can this one be marketed for under $70 when the other is a $175 option?" The public reacted with skepticism as only 3,099 buyers selected the option.

Baldwin/Motion guaranteed mid-11-second quarter-mile times from its Phase III 427 Camaro and was not shy about letting the world know. Motion Performance kingpin Joel Rosen called his line of cars the Fantastic Five.

Another early Funny Car pioneer was Huston Platt, shown here in the 1968 Dixie Twister. In the background is a Tasca Ford Mustang, one of the arch-rivals of the Camaro contingent in drag racing. *Courtesy Drag Racing Memories*

By 1968, the Camaro was also securing a more solid place in the Chevrolet universe. The Camaro was linked with the Corvette in a series of ads and billed as a sort of working man's 'Vette—not a bad position to take. A 1968 Z28 ad claimed the Z was the "Closest thing to a Corvette yet." Chevrolet tried to introduce a nickname for the Camaro, the "Hugger." Ads claimed, "Camaro hugs the road with the best of them. If you've never driven 'The Hugger,' you're in for a big surprise."

The Z28 was also becoming better known. The late introduction and lack of advertising for the Z28 kept the car in the shadows in 1967, but Mark Donohue's success in Trans-Am and word from the drags trip helped bring the car into the sunlight. Changes to the Z28 included an optional rear spoiler, 302 emblems on the leading edge of the fenders, and multi-leaf rear springs. The 302's crankshaft was upgraded with larger main-bearing journal sizes. The price of the option rose to $400. One 1968 Z28 convertible was even built for Pete Estes, general manager for Chevrolet division.

The car magazines were also taking more notice of the Z28. In a 1968 road test, *Road & Track* manhandled a Z through the quarter-mile in 14.9 seconds at 100 miles per hour. "Who says GM isn't racing? If the

Z-28 isn't a bona fide racing car—in street clothing for this test—then we've never seen one," they said. "The engine makes no bones about its character. It idles lumpily at 900 rpm and has very little torque below 4,000 rpm, considering the car's great weight (3,355 pounds)." Above 4,000 rpm, they were more impressed. "Then, hold on! From there it revs so freely it seems it could go on forever."

Car Life also noted its rough-and-tumble nature. "The Z28 Camaro is not cast in the mold of current Detroit space capsules. It is noisy, almost scary in its response to all controls, and delivers a steady barrage of soft blows to the hindsides of its occupants," they wrote. Their testing resulted in a 14.85-second quarter-mile at a fast 101 miles per hour.

Sports Car Graphic editors enjoyed carving corners with the Z28 in their July 1968 issue. "We were most impressed with the handling qualities: the car tracked well, steering was quicker than normal, and most of the rear axle tramp has been eliminated with the help of multi-leaf springs," they wrote. "From a performance standpoint, the 302-cubic inch engine performed much better than any street 327 or 350 we ever drove."

The 1968 Super Sport also benefited from a few changes. There were new SS

1967 Camaro Specifications

	Sport Coupe	Convertible		Sport Coupe	Convertible
Exterior Dimensions (in inches)			*Tire Size and Steering Specifications*		
Wheelbase	108.0	108.0	Standard tire size	7.35x14	7.35x14
Length (overall)	184.7	184.7	Steering ratio, std.	28.0:1	28.0:1
Width (overall)	72.5	72.5	Steering ratio, pwr.	17.5 :1	17.5:1
Height (loaded)	51.4	51.5			
Front tread	59.0	59.0	*Fuel Capacity and Weight*		
Rear tread	58.9	58.9	Rated fuel tank capacity		
			(gallons)	18	18
Interior Dimensions (in inches)			Curb weight		
Head room (frt.)	37.7	38.1	six cyl. (lbs)	2,910	3,165
Head room (rear)	36.5	36.7	Curb weight, V-8 (lbs)	3,070	3,325
Leg room (frt.)	42.5	42.5	Shipping weight		
Leg room (rear)	29.9	29.6	six cyl. (lbs)	2,770	3,025
Hip room (frt.)	56.3	56.3	Shipping weight		
Hip room (rear)	54.5	47.5	V-8 (lbs)	3,020	3,180
Shoulder room (frt.)	56.7	56.7			
Shoulder room (rear)	53.6	47.3			
Entrance height	29.3	29.3			

Yenko Chevrolet spruced up its 427 Camaros, like this 1968 model, with Pontiac Rally wheels, Yenko badges, and a custom fiberglass hood with scoops. For 1968, Yenko produced 64 of the 427-powered Camaros. Yenko later applied the same strategy to the Chevelle and Nova. *Courtesy Greg Rager collection*

stripe choices, and the SS-396 hood had different decoration than the smaller-engined models, with eight chrome "stacks" setting it apart from 1967's simulated vents. A potent option was RPO L89, which added aluminum heads to the 375-horsepower 396. Today, these are prized, as only 272 were so ordered. Like the Z28, SS-350 and SS-396 cars were given multi-leaf rear springs.

The racing season was even better than the year before. Mark Donohue won 8 races in a row in the SCCA's Trans-Am series in a season where he won 10 of 12 races to run away with the manufacturers' title. After finishing fourth at Daytona, he reeled off consecutive wins at Sebring, War Bonnet, Lime Rock, Mid-Ohio, Bridgehampton, Meadowdale, Mt. Tremblant, and Bryar. Later in the year he took wins at Continental Divide and Seattle. Runner-up for the championship was the AMC Javelin driven by George Follmer.

The Trans-Am lore from the Penske/Donohue era remains some of the most compelling in all of racing. With all of

Detroit's manufacturers hoping to fill America's power-crazy, impressionable, young men with lust for their machinery, the competition was especially ruthless. One of the favorite tricks to reduce weight was acid-dipping the car's body, which left the factory sheet metal and silhouette intact, although shaved to a svelte tonnage. The Trans-Am had minimum weight rules, but teams knew that if they stripped their cars to the bone they could add the weight back where it was most advantageous.

Penske had one of his 1967 Camaros dipped at Lockheed Aerospace to the point where the sheet metal was nearly transparent. It caused no end of resentment from competitors and plenty of official scrutiny, but the team still managed to disguise the car and run it again in 1968.

The Camaro's second home was clearly on the drag strip. In the newly formulated Stock Eliminator class of NHRA (formerly Junior Stock), Camaros started winning quickly. Ben Wenzel, in a new B/S-class Camaro,

Some of Yenko's early Camaros were ordered with the COPO 9737 Sports Car Conversion (see chapter 3). This special request through the Chevrolet Fleet and Special Order Department brought the 140-mile per hour speedometer, along with a fatter front sway bar and Goodyear Wide Tread GT tires. With only four miles showing on the odometer, this 1968 COPO 9737 Yenko had barely been run enough to burn the paint off the engine. *Courtesy Greg Rager collection*

The Mr. Bardahl 1968 Camaro takes on General Motors' other favorite among America's youth, the GTO. The GTO, more than any other General Motors car (except the Corvette), hit the youth market target in the bull's-eye in the 1960s. At about the time the GTO was fading in the musclecar relay race, though, the Camaro was there to accept the baton. *Roger Huntington Collection/Dobbs Publishing Group*

took the Nationals event win, pocketing a healthy $4,000 for his troubles. But Bill "Grumpy" Jenkins really set the pace for Camaros in 1967 in Super Stock Eliminator. Jenkins raced his own cars and worked as an engine builder for other racers. He knew his way around a Chevy V-8. His SS/C "Grumpy's Toy III" L78 SS-396 Camaro won the 1967 Super Stock Eliminator championship with mid-11-second time slips, securing the national record in the process. In fact, he was usually holding back, as the car was good for 11-flat time slips.

In 1968, Jenkins ran a 1968 Camaro in Super Stock/C and Super Stock/D, but it was Dave Strickler who won the 1968 NHRA Super Stock World Championship in his "Old Reliable" Z28 Camaro. Strickler, coming out of the North East Division, won the title on October 20, 1968, at the NHRA World Finals in Tulsa, defeating Grumpy Jenkins, his own mechanic.

In the automotive world of the 1960s, body styles changed frequently. The corporations were convinced the public wanted *new*, and they wanted a lot of it. Many cars, especially ponycars, only kept their sheet metal for two or three years. The Camaro was not immune to this philosophy, and thus the original Camaro only lasted for two years before undergoing the stylist's knife—which was a shame. The cleanly-styled first Camaros could easily have lasted longer in the marketplace without looking old. No, they didn't conquer the Mustang in the sales race, but they firmly established that the ponycar could be improved upon and that there was a market for a quarter-million Camaros every year. But Chevrolet was about to prove they could do even better.

Nickey Chevrolet left few doubts about the capabilities of its car. "Nickey Camaro is the heavy-duty street/strip car, has the muscle of a race car but is fully streetable," ads assured. Long before the 427 Camaro became part of Nickey's stable, the dealership had a thriving parts business, as this 1968 ad attests.

Below
If there's anything in the automotive kingdom more intimidating than a Camaro with "427" emblems on the fender, we're waiting to see it. The engine ID was one of the more visible warnings that the Dana Camaro was more than just an everyday musclecar. As a Super Sport with the RS package, this Camaro also sports hideaway headlights. *Mike Mueller*

Left
Dana Chevrolet in South Gate, California, brought its own special talents to the growing industry of creating 427 Camaros. Its optional fiberglass hood, shown here, was distinctive and intimidating. In this case the hood covers an L71 Corvette 427 V-8, rated at 435 horsepower from the factory; although thanks to Dana's optional L88 Phase I cam and dual valve springs, the engine passes more power than that through its lightweight 11-inch clutch. If the orange color doesn't seem familiar, it's because the car was ordered unpainted from Chevrolet and later sprayed at Dana Chevrolet in the bright orange lacquer shown here. *Mike Mueller*

3

The Birth of a Warrior:
1969

Among musclecar enthusiasts, the 1969 Camaro has secured a special place of honor. For starters, the 1969 Camaro stands apart from all other Camaros as a one-year (albeit a long year) body style. But it is also remembered for its position at the top of the heap among fast Camaros, with a vast array of high-performance models and options. Although other Camaros could match some of the 1969's performance features, in no other year was so *much* hardware available.

In 1969, Camaro buyers could choose between Super Sports, Z28s, Rally Sports, Indy Pace Cars, or COPO 427s, equipped with such speed-oriented gear as four-wheel disc brakes, dual four-barrels for the Z28's 302, chambered dual exhaust, aluminum heads for the 396, functional hood scoops, spoilers, Rally wheels, open-element air cleaners, Positraction rear axles with ratios as steep as 4.88:1, heavy-duty M-22 four speeds, and Special Purpose F41 sport suspensions. And if the buyer was so inclined, much of the above was available with a convertible top.

It was all available in a handsome, new body. The overall proportions were the same as before—long hood, short deck—but the 1969 Camaro was 2 inches longer and roughly 1 1/2 inches wider. The larger dimensions gave the Camaro a more aggressive stance, and indeed, the 1969 Camaro was a little less pretty and a little more meaty than the 1967 and 1968 models. The "coke bottle" contours were less pronounced, and two new character lines ran horizontally rearward from the wheel openings. Simulated louvers on the rear quarter panels were more show than go, but all things considered, they were a minor offense.

The interior featured a redesigned instrument panel, with the ignition switch moved to the steering column. The twin round pods for the instruments were gone, replaced by rectangular housings for the gauges, although the optional "special instruments" package still placed the extra gauges down on the console. The larger body opened up some hip and shoulder room. Front seat head restraints became standard equipment. Other functional improvements included variable-ratio steering.

Underhood, the 140-horsepower, 230-inch six-cylinder was still the entry-level engine, with the 155-horsepower, 250-cube six optional. The Torque Drive transmission was again available with the six-cylinder, although for the last time. It was teamed with

The 1969 SS option, when teamed with the Rally Sport package, gave the Camaro a mean visage. The SS group gave the hood stacks, stripes, and SS emblems; the RS equipment provided the hidden headlamps. This SS is equipped with the seldom-seen RPO DX1 hood stripes, a $25.30 option.

Super Sport equipment for 1969 included six chrome hood "stacks." These were introduced on the SS-396 Camaro in 1968 and became standard fare for all SS models in 1969.

The mid-level 396 in 1969 was RPO L34, rated at 350 horsepower. This engine was bracketed on the option list by the entry-level L35 396, rated at 325 horsepower, and the L78 396, rated at 375 horsepower. The L34 shared the 10.25:1 compression ratio of the L35 (the L78 had an 11.0:1 ratio) but had a hotter cam. The L34 was chosen by 2,018 buyers in 1969. All Camaro 396s came with chrome valve covers and open-element air cleaners.

only two axle ratios, 2.73:1 for cars without air conditioning, 3.08:1 for cars with A/C.

The familiar 210-horsepower, 327 V-8 started the model year as the base Camaro V-8 engine, but a new 307-cubic inch V-8 took its place in January 1969. The 307 V-8 was one of the few small-block Chevy incarnations to never be offered in high-performance guise, although it served its purpose as an inexpensive, economical V-8. With two-barrel carburetor and single exhaust it was rated at 200 horsepower. Whereas the 302 Z28 engine was created by fitting the 283 crank in the 327 block, the 307 was created using the reverse formula—the 327 crank in the 283 block. The 307 had a 9.0:1 compression ratio and came with a three-speed manual as its base transmission.

An additional version of the 350 was added to the option list for 1969. Designated the LM1 350, this two-barrel-equipped engine was rated at 255 horsepower. It cost $52.70 over the price of the base V-8. Meanwhile, the 350 four-barrel's output was boosted to 300 horsepower.

The 350 four-barrel remained the standard engine for the 1969 SS. Super Sport equipment that year was similar to that of earlier Super Sports: the 300-horsepower, 350 V-8 with chrome accents, unique side stripes, the special hood with chrome "stacks," hood insulation, external SS emblems and an SS emblem on the steering wheel, 14x7 wheels with F70x14 Wide Oval tires, power disc brakes, a special suspension, the special three-speed manual transmission, and bright accents on the rear fender louvers. It was priced at a bargain $281.

The Rally Sport appearance package continued with a few changes. The most noticeable were the vacuum-operated, slotted headlamp doors, which featured three lenses through which the headlamps peered. The 1969 RS also came standard with new headlamp washers. Other Rally Sport gear included a special grille with an RS emblem, white lenses over amber parking lamps, fender emblems and striping, an RS emblem on the rear panel, and bright accents on the simulated quarter-panel louvers. Interior

features were not much above and beyond the base Sport Coupe—mainly black accents and an RS emblem on the steering wheel. The RS option could be teamed with any engine.

Although clearly no Cadillac Eldorado, a buyer of a 1969 Camaro could create quite the luxurious car. With the extra size and weight, the 1969 Camaro was better suited for comfort than previous models. The Custom Interior included molded vinyl door panels with built-in arm rests, an "assist grip," a carpeted lower panel, woodgrain accents, pedal trim, extra body insulation, a glovebox light, and a mat for the trunk. The extras added $110 to the Camaro's price. Also available were traditional luxuries like

air conditioning, power windows, power steering, and power brakes. The eight-track stereo tape system included four-speakers. Due to the stereo's bulk, if air conditioning was ordered, the tape player was mounted on the center console. The eight-track system was also mounted to the console if the optional gauges were ordered too.

The optional 396 engines were mostly carryover, as was all that engine's charm and all its baggage when installed in the Camaro. As *Car Life* magazine noted in its May 1969 issue following a road test of a 375-horsepower SS-396 Camaro, "The rear axle is a live axle, meaning just what it sounds like. At the mere suggestion of work, the axle leaps and hops, judders and bucks, like the

For 1969, the body color "special front bumper" was a $42.15 option. Early 1969 Z28s did not have the cowl-induction hood, as it was introduced after the regular 1969 introduction. That year the Z28 option cost $458.15.

1969 Z28 Breakdown

The 1969 Z28 package was a $458.15 option. The mandatory power disc brakes and four-speed transmission added $64.25 and $195.40, respectively, to the Sport Coupe's $2,726 base price. By comparison, the 1969 SS package (RPO Z27) cost $295.95, and the RPO Z22 Rally Sport package cost $131.65.

RPO Z28 (Special Performance Package)* included:

- 302-ci, 290-hp V-8
- Dual exhaust with "deep-tone" mufflers
- Special front and rear suspension
- Heavy-duty radiator and temperature-controlled fan
- Quick-ratio steering
- 15x7 Rally wheels
- E70x15 special white lettered tires
- Rear bumper guards
- 3.73:1 axle ratio
- Special Rally stripes on hood and rear deck

* Power disc brakes and four-speed transmission mandatory options

In 1969, the Z28 had its own emblems on the grille and rear body panel. Earlier Z28s were only identifiable by the large twin stripes across the hood and trunk. Rear bumper guards, as shown, were a $12.65 option.

kid who bawls before the switch gets close. Starting, stopping, or turning, whatever the rest of the car wants to do, the rear suspension won't let it do it," they wrote. Wheel hop limited their quarter-mile ETs to a best of 14.77 at 98.72 miles per hour.

They preferred the Camaro's F-car corporate cousin to the SS-396. "The Trans-Am Firebird we drove last month had the same basic body/chassis, similar suspension, and an equally big engine. It had so much lateral grip in back that we couldn't hang the tail out; more power shoved the car off course all right, but in a dependable straight line. Just goes to show, all domestic cars aren't alike. When they are, maybe there'll be a balance between the two extremes displayed by the Camaro and Firebird," they concluded.

But there was one big improvement available for the 396, and that was the L89 aluminum head option. With the aluminum heads installed the engine was rated at the same 375 horsepower as the L78 396, but

the pieces cut roughly 75 pounds off of the 396's weight—all of it from over the front wheels. The L89 option took some detective work to find on the order forms, and at $710 it was one of the most expensive options a Camaro buyer could order. All of which helps explain why only 311 L89 Camaros were built that year, but had Chevrolet promoted the aluminum parts more aggressively, more buyers would have undoubtedly discovered the benefits of the lightweight parts.

Supercars '69 actually got their hands on an L89 SS-396 Camaro with M-22 four-speed, 4.88:1 rear-end gear, and four-wheel discs for a road test. "With the fiberglass-belted street tires smoking and screeching all the way down the quarter, our test Camaro SS-396 was able to rack off times in the low 13s at speeds over 105 miles per hour on every run. This was with absolutely no traction on a slightly damp strip—it had rained the night before—and throwing full-bore power shifts as fast as we could at 6,500 rpm. Our best time slip read 13.00 at 108.62 which is the fastest we've ever recorded for

a factory-stock street machine," they wrote. "These runs were made with closed exhausts and all street equipment in place." They mounted slicks on the rear and cut a 12.62, showing the engine's real potential. "We think Chevrolet should make other tires available with this SS 396/375 package. It's just too much for the stock street treads to handle. Even the optional fiberglass-belted wide treads were useless with so much power under the hood."

Out in the Sunlight

The Z28 really came into its own in 1969, gaining a much higher profile in the public eye. Prominent Z28 emblems joined the twin stripes as identifiers. A couple of months after the regular 1969 new car introduction, a cowl-induction hood with rear air inlet joined the option list, and when ordered with the Z28, these hoods came with "302" engine identification. The Z28 was definitely no longer a racer's secret.

Hot Rod magazine, always on top of the capabilities of the latest Detroit iron, swapped the stock 3.73:1 rear-end gear in

For 1969, the Z28's 302 V-8 used finned-aluminum valve covers in place of the earlier chrome pieces. The Air Injection Reaction (AIR) pump was located under the alternator that year, rather than front and center, as in 1968.

Following pages
Standard SS equipment for 1969 included the 300-horsepower 350-cubic inch V-8, the special hood with chrome stacks, SS striping, hood insulation, F70x14 wide-oval white-letter tires on 14x7 wheels, heavy-duty SS suspension, power disc brakes, a "special" three-speed transmission, trim on the simulated rear quarter louvers, and SS emblems.

Four-wheel disc brakes joined the Camaro factory-option list in 1969. RPO JL8 discs cost $500 when teamed with SS or Z28 equipment. The 11.75-inch rear discs were vented, as were the fronts. Although similar, they were not the same as the Corvette's four-wheel disc brakes. Few Camaros were so equipped. *Roger Huntington Collection/Dobbs Publishing Group*

their test Z28 for a 4.56:1 gear and promptly turned a 14.34-second quarter mile with no other changes. *Hot Rod's* primary interest had always been straight-line performance, but they also were impressed by the Z's handling prowess. "The Z28 can shame some rather expensive machinery without any chassis alteration," they decided. "You can get other super cars for less and plenty that will cut lower ETs, but it'll cost more to get one that goes as quick in a straight or curved line as the Z28 . . . or the 'Cuda."

And the Z28 had some new hardware to show off as well. The most impressive was the dealer-installed, dual four-barrel carburetion setup on a cross-ram manifold. The

Know Your COPO

Among Camaro enthusiasts, the COPO acronym has come to carry as much weight, if not more, than all of the Camaro's other performance-related alpha-numeric codes—Z28, SS-396, IROC, and so on. That's because the COPO letters are understood to designate the mighty 427 Camaro, a car that never officially existed in Chevrolet's regular production pipeline.

COPO itself does not designate a 427 Camaro, but that's how they came about. COPO stands for Central Office Production Order, which was handled out of Chevrolet's Fleet and Special Order Department. Through this channel, buyers of fleet vehicles such as police cars or trucks could order the heavy-duty brakes, larger engines, and unusual parts that were not offered through the regular Chevrolet catalog. The COPO system was also often used for ordering cars painted in colors outside of Chevrolet's offerings; the purchaser of a fleet of Chevy trucks might want his vehicles painted in a Pontiac color to match his business logo, for instance. Once such a change was approved it was given a COPO number and was part of the system.

In the 1960s, General Motors, for safety and image reasons, had a corporate internal policy against intermediate-sized or ponycars having engines larger than 400 cubic inches. Some GM divisions got around this by going to outside suppliers, such as Oldsmobile's partnership with the Hurst corporation, which resulted in the 1969 455-cubic inch Hurst Olds. At the Bow Tie division, performance-minded Chevy dealers went through the COPO network to get around the ban.

The largest available Camaro engine was the 396, but the largest Chevrolet passenger car engine was the 427-inch, big-block V-8. Sold in relatively tame 390-horsepower form under Impala SS hoods and up to 435 horsepower in the Corvette, the 427 seemed like the perfect fit for people who were looking to race the Camaro, whether on the street or strip. Don Yenko was instrumental in getting this 427 Camaro pipeline going. He convinced Chevrolet to build the cars by promising to order 500 of them; whether he actually passed that many through his dealership remains in dispute, but other Chevy

dealers got in on the action too—several hundred COPO 427 Camaros were eventually built.

It appears the 427 Camaros were available in two versions, as outlined below: the L72 cast-iron 427 and the ZL1 aluminum 427. The Tonawanda, New Jersey, production facility built all big-blocks, aluminum and otherwise, as well as many small-blocks.

COPO 9560

This was the designation for the legendary Camaro ZL1 aluminum 427, rated at 430 horsepower. The ZL-1 made its power thanks to an 850-cubic feet per minute Holley double-pumper carburetor, a high-rise aluminum intake manifold with a cut-down plenum chamber, a .560/.600-inch lift solid-lifter cam, and round-port heads. Chevrolet knew the cars were all destined for open headers at the drag strip, but the cars had to be sold with some type of exhaust system in place, so they were fitted with 396 exhaust manifolds running through stock Z28 exhaust pipes and mufflers. The ZL1 427 was backed by an M-22 four-speed transmission and 4.10:1 rear gear. As a badge-less, stripe-delete car, the COPO 9560 had a low-key appearance, although a cowl-induction hood gave notice to keen eyes. The cars were bolstered by heavy-duty springs. The engine package cost $4,160, by itself, easily doubling the price of an SS-396 Camaro. Only 69 were built.

COPO 9561

COPO 9561 was the code for acquiring the cast-iron L72 427 in a Camaro, rated at 425 horsepower. The iron-block 427 was by far the more common of the two 427 Camaros, with several hundred built, although the exact number is still disputed. These, too, had the cowl-induction hoods, heavy-duty suspension, and 12-bolt, Positraction rear ends with either 4.10:1 or 4.56:1 gearing.

COPO 9737–Sports Car Conversion

The COPO sports car conversion, requested first by Don Yenko, brought with it the 140-mile per hour speedometer, Goodyear Wide Tread tires on 15x6 wheels, and a 1-inch front sway bar.

With painted wheels and standard hubcaps, the COPO 427 Camaro looks the picture of innocence. Sharp observers may note the ZL2 "special ducted hood," which was standard equipment with the COPO 427 Camaros. With no external engine identification and standard sport coupe trim, there was little else to give a COPO away, except perhaps the exhaust note. Shown is a COPO 9561, cast-iron L72 Camaro. Mike Mueller

Chevrolet photo shows Z28's optional dual four-barrel carburetion, air cleaner, and "cold air" hood. The unusual intake was cast at the Winters Foundry, and the manifolds are easily recognizable by the snowflake cast onto the manifold. This dealer-installed option provided great top-end power, although low-speed driveability was poor, keeping with its intended use on race tracks. *Roger Huntington Collection/Dobbs Publishing Group*

Mark Donohue put the cap on his championship-winning 1969 season at Riverside in October by winning the final race. It was his sixth win of the season. Better yet for Chevrolet, Camaro driver Ronnie Bucknum finished second. *Bob Tronolone*

Camaro SS Sport Coupe with Super Scoop hood.

GM
MARK OF EXCELLENCE

Camaro's New Super Scoop:
It's like frosting on the frosting.

Basic ingredients, Camaro SS, The Hugger: 300-hp 350 V8. Wide oval treads on 14 x 7 wheels. Beefed-up suspension. Power disc brakes. A floor-mounted 3-speed shifter. Extra topping you can order: A new Super Scoop hood that shoots cooler air to the carburetor for an added dash of dash.

The whole setup works off the accelerator. You step on the gas, it steps up top end power.

There you have it: Super Sport with Super Scoop. Add you and stir.

CHEVROLET

Putting you first, keeps us first.

The "Super Scoop" cowl-induction hood was introduced after the regular 1969 model year rollout. It was standard equipment on Indy Pace Cars and COPO 427 cars and a popular option on Z28s and Super Sports. Its option code was RPO ZL2, and it added $79 to a Camaro's window sticker.

Far left
Shortly after the 1969 Camaro's introduction, the cowl-induction hood joined the option list, and most people, like the buyer of this car, opted for it. The bright Daytona Yellow paint was new for 1969.

Engine displacement emblems for the Z28 were teamed with the cowl-induction hood in 1969. The 302 V-8 was only used from 1967 to 1969 and only advertised on the Z28's exterior the latter two years.

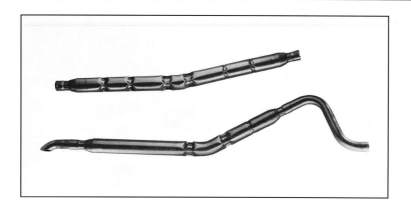

Another feature used on performance Z28 and SS-396 Camaros was the chambered exhaust. Besides offering a healthy growl, the chambered system helped open up the Camaro's restrictive exhaust flow.

dual Holley 600-cubic feet per minute carbs were mated to the cowl-induction hood with a foam seal for better breathing, and for lighter weight, the steel hood could be swapped for a fiberglass one for use with either dual or single carbs. Also available were the optional RPO JL8 rear disc brakes, a $500 option.

Car Life tested the rare combination of dual four-barrels and four-wheel discs for its August 1969 issue. The magazine's below-

average quarter-mile ET of 15.12 at 94.8 miles per hour was largely due to difficulties in getting the peaky engine to launch cleanly. They discovered the dual-quad Z28 was better suited to race tracks than street duty.

"The engine in the test car didn't begin to work until 3,000 [rpm] and didn't develop any power until 5,000," they wrote. "Then the Great Magic Switch has been flipped, and the power comes on with that brassy blaring call to battle that only comes in bottles labeled small-block Chevrolet. But if you wanna fight, go to the road races. Revs for torque is no bargain on the street," they concluded. "The experts told us that the dual carbs were too much for the street, and they were right."

As for the brakes, they were more favorably impressed. "The four-wheel discs made a good braking system better," they decided. "The driver could push very hard without locking the brakes."

Chevrolet took a look at producing even more radical gear for the Z28 Camaro in 1969. The division tasked racing maverick Smokey Yunick with developing aluminum,

Visually impressive, the dual-carb option for the 1969 Z28 also gave a serious boost to top-end power. The twin 600-cubic feet per minute Holleys and manifold added about $500 to the Z28's bottom line. The engine shown here is minus the foam hood-sealing parts.

poly-angle, semi-hemi 302 cylinder heads. Yunick had had a hand in creating several racing Chevrolets, including a Daytona pole-wining 1966 Chevelle and his own 1968 Trans-Am Camaro. Known as an innovator, Yunick took the job to heart and developed the heads into running prototypes. Visually impressive, the heads never produced the power Yunick and Chevrolet were looking for, and the effort was dropped.

If the level of performance equipment offered for the Camaro seemed excessive (okay, it was), Chevrolet was only keeping up with the Joneses. By 1969, the competition had gotten fiercer. Ford offered the Mustang in Mach 1 (which had the 428 Cobra Jet as an option), Boss 429, Shelby GT-350, GT-500, and GT trim. The Mercury Cougar was available with Boss 302, 351 4-V, 390, or 428 CJ engines. The Plymouth Barracuda was sold with the impressive 340- or 383-inch V-8s, plus a few 440s that snuck out the door. The AMC Javelin and AMX offered a 390-cubic inch V-8, and Pontiac's own Firebird had sprouted wings with a Ram Air 400 engine and a handling-oriented Trans-Am model. And those were just the other ponycars. The intermediates were something else entirely. Mopars were infested with 426 Hemi and 440 Six-Pack big-blocks, Hurst was making a special edition 455-inch Oldsmobile, and Ford had pushed aside its 390-cube V-8 in the Fairlane in favor of the 428 Cobra Jet.

On top of all that, the Z28's first serious competitor in Trans-Am racing hit the field in 1969. Ford's Boss 302 Mustang was the new prototype for Trans-Am racing sedans. The Boss engine used a canted-valve design, with huge ports for high-end breathing and four-bolt mains for strength. Like the Z28's 302, the Boss was rated at 290 horsepower and 290 pounds-feet of torque. Its suspension was similarly oriented toward carving up curvy road courses.

After receiving the COPO 427 Camaros from Chevrolet, Yenko installed headers and Yenko SC 427 identification. The L72 427 benefited from the cowl-induction hood that came standard with the COPO Camaros, as it provided fresh, cold air pulled in from the low-pressure area at the cowl.

Following pages
Yenko Chevrolet's 1969 sYc Camaros were given distinctive Yenko striping in a pattern shared with the dealer's 427-powered Chevelles and Novas. As COPO cars, all 1969 Yenko Camaros came with the cowl-induction hood. The Rallye Green model pictured stickered for $4,700 when new, although it sold for considerably less.

Z is for "Zap!"
Translation: a 302 V8 with mechanical lifters, hi-perform-ance cam, aluminum intake manifold, Holley 4-barrel.
Plus: multi-leaf rear springs, heavy-duty shocks, new white-lettered tires on 15 x 7 wheels.
And a Hurst shifter for the 4-speed.
While you're at it, why not add the new 'Vette type 4-wheel disc brakes?
By now you know the mean streak isn't just painted on—it's built in.
Putting you first, keeps us first.

We've got a mean streak.

Z/28 Camaro.

No longer a semi-secret option ordered only by those in the know, the Z28 Camaro came roaring out of the closet illuminated by the full light of Chevrolet advertising in 1969. Ads were remarkably free of hype, instead focusing on the important technical features of the Z.

The new competition was tough, but the Camaro packed the ultimate nuclear deterrent for those in the know. Through the Central Office Production Order (COPO) system (see sidebar), Chevrolet produced a handful of 427-powered Camaros. For dealers and racers who knew the ins and outs of ordering fleet vehicles, Camaros with the Corvette's 425-horsepower 427 and the all-aluminum ZL-1 427 were available. This made things considerably easier for the dealer/converters like Yenko Chevrolet, who then no longer had to perform engine swaps to create a 427 Camaro.

Although shrouded in mystery for years after the fact, these radical Camaros nearly reached regular production status. Development engineer Chuck Hughes remembered the ZL-1s on the proving ground. "The ones that we loved were the 396 and 427 aluminum-block and aluminum-head jobs," he

recalled. "Now *that* was a piece of work. That was fun. We had a lot of prototypes around with that. You had weight about like the small-block, but with torque like the large block.

"We always had them around and had them on test trips and said, 'Should we do it?' No one seemed to be as aggressive at going after aluminum parts on an engine at that time," he said. The reasons included the high cost of an all-aluminum engine, especially in the limited volumes such a car would likely sell.

One business that was aggressive about the ZL-1 Camaro was Fred Gibb Chevrolet. The performance-minded dealership ordered 50 ZL-1 Camaros for racing, and they were a terror on the drag strip with drivers like Dick Harrell at the helm. Other dealers, most notably Berger Chevrolet, ordered 19 additional ZL-1s in 1969.

The 1969 Yenko Camaros combined two Chevrolet COPO (Central Office Production Order) requests to good effect. The COPO 9737 Sports Car Conversion provided the 140-mile per hour speedometer, sport suspension, and Rally wheels. COPO 9561 provided the L72 427.

Cars magazine actually wrangled a road test of a ZL-1 Camaro. Although its editors acknowledged the ZL-1s were built to race, they also wanted to test the car in as close to street trim as possible. They recorded a 13.16 quarter mile at 110.21 miles per hour. "The ZL-1 camshaft was definitely smooth enough to drive on the street, at least in warm weather, though the idle was quite rough," they commented. "One sober note was that the rich-jetted 850-cubic feet per minute Holley carb gave only 5 to 7 miles per gallon in normal street driving! But when you jump on that loud pedal, all is forgiven!"

The main detriment, and one reason why only professional racers ended up with the cars, was price. Their test ZL-1 from Berger Chevrolet stickered out at $7,800, or roughly twice the price of an L78 SS-396 coupe. The engine package alone cost $4,100!

The single biggest outlet for COPO 427 Camaros was Yenko Chevrolet, which was better known for selling the iron-block 427s. Where previously he had swapped 427s under Camaro hoods to create his sYc Camaros, for 1969 he swung a deal with Chevrolet to order them factory-direct. It was a much better deal for all involved.

Don Yenko explained the advantages to interviewer Greg Rager, in an article

Although the available records show 201 1969 Yenko 427 Camaros were built, the late Don Yenko (at left) and a few others placed the number, by memory, at 500. Photographs such as this, showing a ceremony for the 350th car built, have added to the confusion.

One of the most wonderfully belligerent advertisements of the musclecar era was this Camaro and Corvette challenge to the other cars in the magazine. No other manufacturer packed this kind of one-two punch. Who could respond? AMC with an AMX and a Rambler?

published in the April 1987 issue of *Musclecar Review*: "The most significant difference was the warranty issue," he related. "In 1967 and 1968, I had to cover the cars with my own warranty, with no backing from the factory at all. The 1969 COPO cars, of course, had a full factory warranty. GM didn't do this for nothing; I had to pay them a lot of money to warranty the cars, but it did turn out to be cheaper in the long run."

In the end, at least for Yenko, acquiring the 427 Camaros turned out to be easier than selling them. As Yenko explained to *Musclecar Review,* "We did extremely well for about the first eight months of the year, then the insurance companies caught up with us and started flatly refusing to insure the cars at any amount of money. This turned the last 100 or so cars into really distressed merchandise. We had a heck of a time selling them," he said.

While other power-minded dealers were turning to COPO 427s for their ultimate Camaros, Baldwin/Motion was still performing engine swaps tailored to the customer's wishes. Baldwin/Motion even out-did the factory COPO system toward the end of the 1969 model run. "There were a couple of '69 Camaros that were late Camaros that got out with 454s," Motion Performance honcho Joel Rosen recalled.

On Track

With seemingly every performance option in Chevy's arsenal available in the Camaro, 1969 was a good year for Camaro street performance. It was also another good year for the Camaro on the race tracks of North America.

Mark Donohue won the SCCA Trans-Am series again after a fierce duel with Parnelli Jones' Boss 302 Mustang. Donohue's six wins were enough to clinch the title for Chevrolet, 156 points to 130. He won at Bryar, Mt. Tremblant, Watkins Glen, Laguna Seca, Sears Point, and Riverside. And Donohue wasn't the only Camaro racer to find his way to the winner's circle. Ronnie Bucknum scored a pair of Trans-Am wins in a 1969 Penske Camaro.

The Penske Z28s, in particular, have secured a hallowed place in racing lore. The acid dipping given some of the Penske Camaros to reduce weight resulted in paper thin sheet metal, and the roofs tended to buckle and ripple under racing conditions, potentially giving the advantage away. Penske disguised this by fitting some of the 1969s with *vinyl tops*. SCCA officials were not amused, and other competitors protested the disguised sheet metal, but Penske maintained they were to set the Sunoco cars apart from the pack—which they surely did. Besides, there was no regulation against vinyl tops.

But it wasn't just creative interpretation of the rules that kept the Penske vehicles in front. Donohue really was that good a driver (he would win the Indianapolis 500 in 1972), and the Penske operation was nothing if not first class. A dissection of the 1969 Penske racers shows a blueprint for the Camaro Z28 taken to its logical, maximum extreme. The Traco-built, blueprinted 302 V-8 ran somewhere north of 440 horsepower thanks to the dual four-barrels on a cross-ram intake, Traco valvetrain, a 12.0:1 compression ratio, and, of course, Sunoco 103-octane Super Premium. The chassis was stiffened with a roll cage and braking up-

When the Camaro was selected to pace the Indianapolis 500 for the second time in three years, Chevrolet was a lot more serious about marketing a commemorative model. The RPO Z11 Indy Sport Convertible Accents was a regular option, teamed with the SS/RS packages and Hugger Orange stripes over Dover White paint. Chevrolet found 3,675 buyers that year.

Standard fare with all 1969 Pace Car convertibles was the orange houndstooth interior. The car pictured has the optional tilt steering column ($45.30) and woodgrain plastic steering wheel ($34.80).

graded to Corvette 11.75-inch discs, with an adjustable proportioning valve. The handling benefited from all manner of tweaks designed to improve camber and lower the car's center of gravity, plus Koni adjustable shocks, stiffer bushings, large roll bars, and Goodyear Blue Streak racing tires on 9-inch-wide Minilite wheels.

The Camaro was also still a force on the nation's drag strips. Baldwin/Motion Camaros were tearing up NHRA A/Modified production, and the New York-based speed shop was a multiple national record holder in its Camaro. "We were swapping the record around with our Camaro between us and [Grumpy] Jenkins," Motion's Rosen recalled.

Jenkins may well have been the highest-profile Camaro drag racer of them all in 1969. His "Grumpy's Toy" 427 Camaro was the first in its class to break into the nines. Jenkins switched to a 1970 Camaro the following year and added to his success later in the decade with a succession of Vegas and Monzas.

Indy Pace Car coupes and convertibles were equipped with the cowl-induction hood, or "Super Scoop" hood, as it was advertised. The 350 four-barrel V-8 was rated at 300 horsepower for 1969. Hood insulation was part of the SS package.

1969 Camaro Specifications

Slightly larger than the 1967–1968 Camaros, the 1969 models were nonetheless still trim, lithe ponycars by the standards of the day. Listed are the car's vital statistics:

	Sport Coupe	Convertible
Exterior Dimensions (in inches)		
Wheelbase	108.0	108.0
Length (overall)	186.0	186.0
Width (overall)	74.0	74.0
Height (loaded)	51.6	51.5
Front tread	59.6	59.6
Rear tread	59.5	59.5
Interior Dimensions (in inches)		
Head room (frt.)	37.0	37.5
Head room (rear)	36.7	36.8
Leg room (frt.)	42.5	42.5
Leg room (rear)	29.2	29.5
Hip room (frt.)	56.3	56.3
Hip room (rear)	54.6	47.5
Shoulder room (frt.)	56.5	56.5
Shoulder room (rear)	53.6	47.3
Entrance height	29.2	29.4
Tire Size and Steering Specifications		
Standard tire size	E78x14	E78x14
(SS)	F70x14	F70x14
Steering ratio, std.	27.3:1	27.3:1
Steering ratio, pwr.	15.5:1–11.8:1	15.5:1–11.8:1
Fuel Capacity and Weight		
Rated fuel tank capacity (gallons)	18	18
Curb weight, six (lbs)	3,005	3,255
Curb weight, V-8 (lbs)	3,145	3,395
Shipping weight six (lbs)	2,910	3,160
Shipping weight V-8 (lbs)	3,050	3,300

Available Colors, 1969

Solid colors ....Code		Solid colors ....Code	
Tuxedo Black	10	Burgundy	67
Dover White	50	Cortez Silver	69
Glacier Blue	53	Garnet Red	52
Dusk Blue	51	Champagne	63
Le Mans Blue	71	Fathom Green	57
Olympic Gold	65	Butternut Yellow	40
Burnished Brown	61	Hugger Orange	72
Azure Turquoise	55	Daytona Yellow	76
Frost Green	59	Rallye Green	79

Available Two-Tone Combinations
Glacier Blue (lower) & Dover White (upper)
Azure Turquoise (lower) & Dover White (upper)
Glacier Blue (lower) & Dusk Blue (upper)
Dusk Blue (lower) & Glacier Blue (upper)
Olympic Gold (lower) & Dover White (upper)
Burnished Brown (lower) & Champagne (upper)

Little known even today, Chevrolet also offered Indy Pace Car accents for the Camaro coupe, tagged Z10. Information on these cars is sketchy, but most seem to have been marketed in the Midwest and Southwest where, due to weather extremes, a convertible made less sense. The 1969 Coupes did not come with "Official Pace Car" decals installed from the factory.

Rally Sport interior equipment in 1969 included an RS emblem on the steering wheel, but if the SS and RS packages were combined, the SS emblems took precedence. Beyond steering wheel insignia, there was little else to distinguish the RS or SS interior from that of the standard Camaro sport coupe. Most of the SS and RS gingerbread was on the outside. Ordering RPO Z87 Custom Interior netted the buyer woodgrain accents on the dash and the "Custom" all-vinyl interior.

Rear treatment for the Super Sport included chunky SS badges on rear panel and trim moldings for the rear quarter louvers. Teaming the SS option with the Rally Sport Package provided for separate back-up lamps installed below the bumper. Rear bumper guards were available separately or as part of an Appearance Guard Group, which included front and rear bumper guards, door edge guards, floor mats, and a visor vanity mirror.

The Camaro also played a part in the biggest race of them all in 1969, the Indianapolis 500. The Camaro was chosen to be the pace car again, the second time in three years. Jim Rathmann, the race winner in 1960, was the pace car driver, while Mario Andretti went on to win the race. Naturally, Chevy celebrated with a pace car replica for street use. Indy Pace Cars were all SS Rally Sports, equipped with cowl-induction hoods, Rally wheels, and a unique color combination of Hugger Orange stripes over Dover White paint. The cars had Orange Houndstooth interiors. The number of 1969 Pace Car replicas dwarfed the number of 1967 festival cars produced, as 3,675 convertible replicas were built, plus an undetermined number of Pace Car coupes. Two Pace Car replicas were built for Canadian consumption.

As Chevrolet experienced delays getting the next heavily-revised Camaro to market, the 1969 body style stayed in production until late 1969. The extended model year helped the 1969 Camaro become the best selling of the first-generation cars, plus established an enduring mystique. The new cars arrived on February 26, 1970, and were well received. But after a 12-year run, those Camaros lost a lot of their luster. Not so with the 1969s—they stood apart then and still do today.

At the top of the musclecar mountain, where the air and the dollars get quite rare, sits the ZL-1 COPO Camaro. With an all-aluminum 427 Corvette V-8, laughably rated for public consumption at 430 horsepower, the ZL-1 offered big-block power with small-block weight. Only 69 were built, so its reputation comes more from legend than actual encounters on the street, but with slicks and open exhaust it was realistically an 11-second quarter-miler. *Mike Mueller*

The all-aluminum ZL-1 427 was installed in two Corvettes in 1969, but 69 of the pricey engines were installed in Camaros thanks to the COPO pipeline. Output was rated at 430 horsepower, although 500-plus was more like it. One distinguishing characteristic of the ZL-1's engine compartment is the crooked neck on the heavy-duty Harrison radiator.

When it became evident the upcoming, redesigned 1970 Camaro was not going to be ready for the fall 1969 new-car introduction, Chevrolet released this photo of the 1969 Camaro wearing 1970 plates. Later, Chevrolet decided to keep the 1969 model in production through the end of the year as a 1969 model and give the 1970 Camaro a midyear introduction as a 1970 model once the calendar page had turned. *Detroit Public Library National Automotive History Collection*

Bill "Grumpy" Jenkins was one of the top Camaro racers in the late 1960s. His "Grumpy's Toy" series of Chevys were regular winners, and he also built engines for other successful drivers. He turned full-time professional racer in the late 1960s and enjoyed a long career in the Stock and Pro Stock ranks through the 1970s and 1980s. Shown is his 1969 SS, catching some air under the front wheels. The 1969 Camaro may be the most successful model in NHRA history, with 124 National event wins from 1969 to 1998. Through 1998, Camaros of all years have won 369 victories in NHRA competition. *Courtesy Drag Racing Memories*

The Working Man's Ferrari:
1970-1981

If the 1967 Camaro was what a lot of people expected it to be, the 1970 Camaro was something no one anticipated. When it was introduced in February 1970, jaws dropped. *This* was a Chevrolet? The styling was much more exotic than any previous American sporty coupe and certainly more radical than anything this price range had seen before. Hell, even the Corvette looked like no big thing next to the 1970 Camaro.

The new Camaro featured mostly familiar powertrains under the pretty new skin, but the chassis and suspension were certainly improved, so there was substance to go with the style. But it was the looks that astounded people. And that was the intention all along. Bill Mitchell was GM design vice president during the car's development and wanted a Camaro that was more like a true sports car and less like an altered sedan. Dave Holls, as Chevrolet group chief designer, and Henry Haga, still at Chevrolet Number 2 Studio during the car's inception, worked over several design themes in as much secrecy as they could muster. Work on the 1970 Camaro had started almost as soon as the 1967 Camaro was born, with the Pontiac studio under Bill Porter also laboring on the 1970 Firebird.

In the end, much of the Pontiac team's work influenced the final F-car design, although both divisions created as much of a distinct personality for their respective cars as common platforms and parts allowed. Both were a smashing success from a design standpoint, and people noticed. Development engineer Chuck Hughes remembered the public reaction at a press introduction in California prior to the Camaro's public introduction. He, Chassis Engineer Bob Dorn, and Dave McLellan went out in public with three prototypes and were promptly surrounded.

"That was when Sunset Strip was not quite as bad as it is today. It was more where everybody went out at night," Hughes said. "I remember that we drove down the street a couple of times in the cars, and we were mobbed. There was a *ton* of young people that came out and stopped us in the street and wanted to see the car. So we just stopped and opened the hood, the doors, the whole works. There must have been 100 kids around there looking at the cars."

The new Camaro didn't just turn on car-crazy southern California. Nearly everyone in the car world noted the car's international flavor. Back North, the snowbound staff at *Car and Driver* were driven to rare fits of gushing. "It would be every bit as much at home on the narrow, twisting streets of Monte Carlo or in the courtyard of a villa overlooking the Mediterranean as it is on Interstate 80. It's a Camaro like none before," they judged.

At *Road & Track,* they also noticed the public's interest. "We got our test car about a week before public introduction and greatly enjoyed the reactions of people on the streets to it. Some practically crashed into trees gawking at its European snout and graceful lines, but we got the feeling several times that drivers of older Camaros were purposely ignoring it. Did they feel abandoned, or did they simply not realize it was a Camaro?"

If there was a criticism of the new design (one that became increasingly apparent as the cars aged), it was the long, heavy doors. Although the doors contained side impact beams and eliminated rear quarter windows for some cost savings, the weight of

The SS option survived the change of bodies in 1970. As before, the blacked-out grille was part of the package. The single-bar bumper was standard with the SS; ordering the Rally Sport option brought the split bumper.

the doors tended to strain the hinges, and Camaro's doors often sagged after a time. Also, no convertible was offered, although one had been mocked-up in the studios. Decreasing sales of convertibles, along with anticipated new government regulations, ended those plans.

Chevrolet seriously considered producing a "Kammback" station wagon Camaro. Although hard to visualize now, the concept was not completely without precedent. Volvo produced a two-door station wagon off their P1800E sport car platform, a car that was not without charm. And Chevrolet had trotted out the concept before, with its "Nomad" Corvette show car of 1954. Ultimately for cost reasons, the Camaro wagon was never green-lighted for production, although the idea continued to surface at GM throughout the 1970s. Pontiac even produced a Trans-Am wagon show car late in the decade.

As mentioned earlier, the new Camaros were functionally much improved as well. Alex Mair served as director of engineering during the car's development. Some of the improvements shepherded through included moving the steering mechanism ahead of the front axle centerline, which gave the Camaro more controllable understeer, along with some improvements in crash safety and serviceability. The 1970 Camaro had a stronger front subframe and twin roof panels, which created a stiffer body structure and led to a quieter interior. Wider treads also contributed to handling ability, and standard 11-inch front disc brakes meant even the entry-level cars had the best braking available.

The powertrain line-up was largely carryover, with a few new twists. The 230-inch six was dropped, leaving the 250-inch six as the base engine. The 307 was the entry-level V-8, with the 350-cubic inch two-barrel and four-barrel V-8s as the upgrades. The L35, 325-horsepower, 396 V-8 was left off the option list, leaving only the 350-horsepower and 375-horsepower versions of the engines. The 396-inch big-block available in 1970 had actually been bored out to 402

The 1970 Camaro jumped a full generation ahead of its competitors with its European-inspired design. But small touches, such as the round taillights, were intended to maintain a family resemblance to other Chevrolets, notably the Corvette. Shown is a Rally Sport model. *Detroit Public Library National Automotive History Collection*

cubic inches but was never advertised as such. Evidently there was still some marketing magic left in the 396 designation.

But the big news centered around the Z28. The old high-revving 302 was gone, replaced by the LT-1 350. The LT-1 350 used in the Z28 retained many of the 302 characteristics: it was tuned right to the ragged edge where reasonable street manners duke it out with cranky race-track abilities. The engine was rated at 370 horsepower in the Corvette and 360 horsepower when installed in the Camaro Z28, due to a slightly more restrictive exhaust.

Read the spec sheet, and it's easy to see why the LT-1 was so powerful and durable. The block featured four-bolt mains, and the reciprocating assembly consisted of a forged steel crank and TRW pistons that produced an 11.0:1 compression ratio. The engine breathed through an aluminum intake manifold and 780-cubic feet per minute Holley carburetor.

The solid-lifter cam was a stout grind, and the cylinder heads housed large 2.02-inch intake valves and 1.60-inch exhaust valves. Other features included a high-performance oil pump, aluminum valve covers, and a chrome air cleaner cover. In another departure from Z28s past, the 1970 Z was the first to be available with an automatic transmission, although air conditioning was still not available with Chevy's top Camaro.

The 1970 edition was the fastest Z28 yet. *Car and Driver*'s road test numbers in May 1970 showed a quarter mile of 14.2 seconds at 100 miles per hour. "The automatic transmission test car had a little help from a 4.10-to-1 axle ratio, not exactly what we would have dialed up of our own free will. The surprising thing is that the high-winding gear is relatively tolerable in this speed-limited United States, provided you're not short of gas money," they wrote. "If you're interested in acceleration, however, the

Standard SS equipment in 1970 was much as it was in 1969: the 350-cubic inch V-8; SS emblems on the grille, fenders, and steering wheel; hood insulation; power brakes; and 14x7-inch wheels. When the big-block was ordered, 396 engine identification replaced the 350 badges. One new feature was the hideaway windshield wipers. This car has been painted with Z28 stripes.

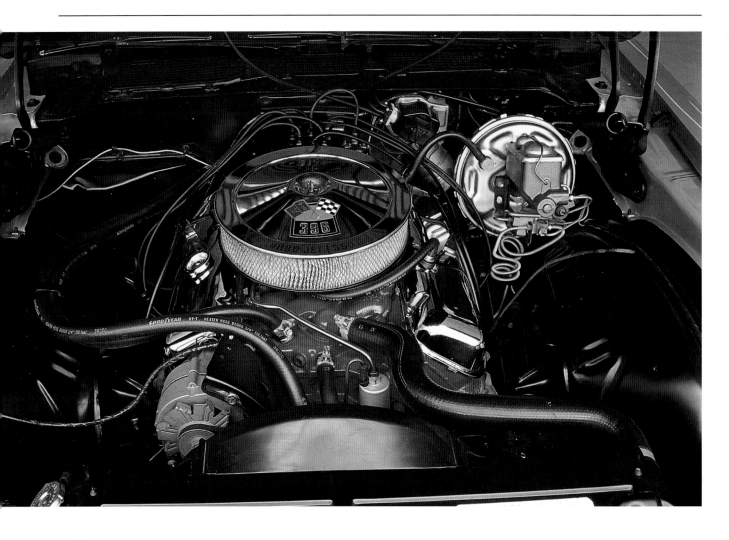

Z28, despite its increase in muscle, is still soft on the low end and with the automatic it would probably bog with a lesser gear."

Motorcade posted a 14.5 at 98 miles per hour in its Z28 test car. By comparison, *Road Test* magazine coaxed an SS-396 with a four-speed transmission and 3.31:1 rear axle ratio to a 15.3-second quarter mile at 92.7 miles per hour in its August 1970 issue. *Road & Track* sampled a 1970 SS Rally Sport with a 300-horsepower 350 in May 1970 and clocked a quarter mile of 16.6 seconds at 86 miles per hour.

Public notice and press accolades were great, but the 1970 Camaro didn't score on every front. In SCCA Trans-Am racing it was not a great year for Camaro. After securing back-to-back championships in 1968 and 1969, Roger Penske and Mark Donohue jumped ship to a suddenly aggressive AMC in 1970. Fielding Javelins, Donohue won three races that year and nearly won the championship for AMC. With the well-oiled Penske team leaving Chevrolet behind, it

was rough going for the Camaro, but there were other well-run teams that stepped in to fill the gap. Owens-Corning sponsored Tony DeLorenzo in a Camaro, and Jim Hall's Chaparral Racing fielded a pair of 1970 Z28s for Hall and Ed Leslie. But it was independent Milt Mintner who took a 1969 Camaro to victory at Donnybrooke, and Vic Elford who scored a late-season win in a Camaro at Watkins Glen. It was a far cry from the Donohue steamroller of years past, though, and Parnelli Jones won the season title in a Boss 302 Mustang.

Camaros were shut out of Trans-Am victory lane in 1971 and 1972, and by the mid-1970s the Corvette had become the Trans-Am racer of choice. But, while shaped like a European exotic, the early 1970s Camaros were still powered by Chevy V-8s, and they continued to clean up at the drag strip. Baldwin/Motion remained a leader, and with Dennis Ferrara as driver, it secured the NHRA A/Modified championship from 1971 to 1973. Grumpy Jenkins had an up-and-down year with his 1970 Pro Stock Camaro but was still able to win select events.

Slow Leak

For a lot of reasons, 1970 is often remembered as the last great year for American musclecars. There was a new Camaro and Firebird, a new Dodge Challenger and Plymouth Barracuda, and several freshly restyled intermediate musclecars. At GM, the 427-inch, big-block V-8 gave way to the 454, and 455-cubic inch V-8s were finally lowered into GTOs, 442s, and Buick Gran Sports. Chrysler still had the 426 Hemi and 440 Six-Pack, and Ford produced both 428 Cobra Jets *and* Boss 429s. Mark Donohue even put his name on the spoiler of a special-edition AMC Javelin. It was either hot rod heaven on Earth or the pinnacle of irresponsible excess, depending on which side of the aisle you sat.

But the pressure on auto makers had been building for quite some time. The Environmental Protection Agency was formed shortly after the 1970 Camaro hit the road, and insurance companies were making it harder for young people to buy the high-powered machinery they lusted after. Among the first mandates from the government was the phasing out of leaded gasoline and a dramatic lowering of auto exhaust emissions.

In this, General Motors was a leader. For 1971 they were the first to lower compression ratios on all the corporation's engines. The 1971s were also set up to run leaner

The 1970 Camaro's interior offered more of a wraparound dash design, a marked improvement over the 1969 model's flat, vertical design. The woodgrain accents on the dash were part of the interior accent group (RPO Z23) and the Z87 Custom Interior. As the 1970s progressed, fake wood crept like kudzu through the interiors of many American cars, providing that extra touch of leisure-suit class.

The optional RPO D80 one-piece spoiler, as on this car, was used on the 1970 Camaros but was later replaced by a taller three-piece spoiler. The spoiler was a $32 option.

Most Rally Sport equipment consisted of exterior trim in 1970, although an RS emblem on the steering wheel was a constant reminder for the driver. Other RS doodads included the split front bumpers, blacked-out grille, repositioned license-plate bracket, hideaway wipers, assorted bright body moldings, and Rally Sport nameplates on the fenders. *Roger Huntington Collection/Dobbs Publishing Group*

Chevrolet played up the Camaro's clean and exciting styling after the car's 1970 introduction. "You get the impression that it's a driver's car from the ground up."

than previously. Although friendlier to the country's air, dropping compression ratios and leaning out the fuel mixture had the expected effect on performance, which is to say, bad. The Z28's LT-1 350 was detuned from an 11.0:1 compression ratio to 9.0:1, with horsepower dropping from 360 to 330. Other Camaro V-8 compression ratios were cut to 8.5:1, which dropped the 396's (that is, the 402's) horsepower rating to 300.

As Chevrolet engineers wrestled with lower compression ratios, many ideas were proposed to keep the Z28 competitive. One such idea included producing a 400-inch, small-block Z28. With 400 cubic inches, Chevrolet might make up in displacement what was lost in compression, while still keeping the lower weight of the small-block. After all, Ford and Chrysler had held out on dropping compression ratios on their high-performance engines, so Ford still had high-compression Mach 1s, Boss 351s, and a 429 SCJ. Dodge and Plymouth still offered the 426 Hemi, 440 six-barrel, and 440 four-barrel in high-compression tune.

But the 400 was never approved, and it probably would not have made any difference had it been given the thumbs-up anyway. Once sales for 1971 were tallied, it was evident the bottom had fallen out of the performance market, and Ford, Chrysler, and AMC quickly followed the low-compression road in 1972. (Although sales were poor in the early 1970s, the seeds of future recovery were planted when the Federal excise tax on automobiles was repealed in April 1971.)

How did the new engine settings affect performance on the street? In 1971 *Hot Rod* magazine tested a 300-horse SS-396 Camaro and recorded a 14.827 quarter mile. Not bad, really, but they obviously missed the horsepower. "Given a list of equipment like a 396-cubic inch V-8, four-speed transmission, 3.42:1 Positraction rear, all packaged into an SS Camaro, there would seem to be no doubt that this is a top-of-the-line musclecar. On paper it is; on a drag strip it isn't," they wrote. *Car and Driver*'s sequel to its 1970 Z28 road test yielded numbers even more discouraging. The 1971 four-speed Z28 was only good for a 15.1 quarter mile.

"All this means that the days of the solid-lifter Z28 that we've all known and loved are numbered. It will survive this year and maybe next, but it will never make 1975. Fortunately, in packaging the engine, Chevrolet has learned a great deal about building successful sporty cars,"

they concluded. "Only the Pontiac Trans-Am, a sister under the skin, is in the same league."

They could make that claim because, for once, Ford had taken a major misstep. The Mustang, once the lightest, cutest partner at the ponycar square dance, had grown into a chunky Clydesdale. Although still fast, thanks to Boss 351 and 429 powerplants, the car had thick rear-end bodywork and a "flatback" design that offered almost no visibility. It was too large and too heavy, and people who loved the original weren't smitten by this new version.

Given all that, the Camaro was surely one of the best cars of its type available in North America, but nonetheless, performance was down, sales were down, and the news was about to get worse. Continuing labor unrest led to a prolonged strike at the Norwood, Ohio, factory in 1972. The strike lasted from April to September, crippling 1972 production and delaying the ramp-up of the 1973 models. It was then that the Camaro story very nearly came to an end.

The combination of the strike, lower sales, and impending bumper crash-worthiness regulations that were going to force a front-end redesign nearly pushed Chevrolet to cancel the Camaro. Fortunately there were several inside the company who championed the car's cause,

among them were Chevrolet chief engineer Alex Mair and a strong contingent of advocates from the Pontiac side. One way in which the Camaro team stayed the car's execution was to develop an inexpensive solution to the stricter bumper requirements for the 1973 models.

As for the 1972 models themselves, they were little changed from the year before. They had a new grille pattern and slicker-looking vinyl tops. Camaros may have been getting slower, but at least they were also getting safer. In 1971, high-back bucket seats were installed, and in 1972, three-point safety belts were incorporated.

Although more realistic net horsepower figures first surfaced at GM in 1971, they were introduced alongside the old gross figures that year. For 1972 the net figures were all that were released. The net ratings were calculated by dyno testing the engines with engine accessories in place, whereas the old gross ratings were figured with the engines set up in much more free-breathing form than they would be in production cars. For 1972, that translated into a Z28 with 255 horsepower at 5,600 rpm and a 396 with 240 horses underhood.

Road & Track tested the 1972 Z28 for its April 1972 issue. The magazine's Z28, one with automatic transmission and 4.10

gearing, turned the quarter mile in 15.5 seconds at 90 miles per hour. By comparison, a 350 two-barrel car with four-speed manual transmission ran a 17.2 quarter mile at 82.5 miles per hour. They liked the 350 two-barrel Camaro, praising its refinement and economy. "The two-barrel equipped 350-cubic inch V-8 and four-speed turned out to be a most satisfactory combination, quiet and at least acceptably smooth for a 1972 emission-controlled engine. There was some evidence of the carburetion leanness . . . especially at low speeds and light throttle," they

noted, echoing a familiar criticism of early emission-controlled engines.

For 1973, the redesigned bumpers that had been in the works so long were put into production. They were more sturdily reinforced and featured vertical bumper guards on the front. Remarkably, considering the new bumper standards, the engineers managed to keep the Rally Sport's split bumpers and protruding grille alive for 1973, although for the last time.

The Z28 continued its crash course in civility. The 1973 edition was the first to be available with air conditioning. The old solid-lifter cam was replaced with a milder grind and hydraulic lifters, and a more pedestrian cast-iron intake manifold was substituted for the aluminum part used previously. Horsepower was factored at 245.

The Z28 survived, but other old Camaro friends were not so lucky. The SS option was retired for 1973, as was the 396 big-block engine. Not quite so badly missed was the two-speed Powerglide transmission, which was finally sent to the glue factory. But with the cancellation of the 396, the 350-cubic inch V-8 was the largest available Camaro engine. Interestingly, while Chevrolet had been selling fewer and fewer big-block Camaros, finally dropping the option, Pontiac had been traveling in the opposite direction. The Trans-Am was beefed up with the 455-cubic inch V-8 in 1971, and Pontiac continued to sell the mega-motor option through 1976. Pontiac even managed to keep the 400 V-8 in service through 1979, long after Chevrolet had given up on big-inch Camaros. Although few 455s were sold in the early 1970s, Pontiac's performance image was kept alive, much to its advantage later in the decade.

Taking the place of the departed SS was a new luxury-oriented model, the Type LT. The Type LT came standard with rocker panel trim and painted lower body, dual outside mirrors, rally wheels, extra sound deadener, LT emblems, and Sport instrumentation. Buyers could combine the Z28 and Rally Sport options with the Type LT for a true luxury/sport Camaro. Adding to the relatively luxurious nature of the car was the return of power windows to the option list, which had been missing since 1969. The power window switches were mounted in the center console, requiring that option. The LT was quite a popular model and helped spark an upward trend in Camaro sales. After surviving all manner of ills, the Camaro had finally bottomed out, and sales were on their way back up.

454 CAMARO... *The Mean Machine*

Tune into what's happening at Baldwin/Motion supercar diggers and pick up on what we're laying down. Plymouth may have a 'System'; Olds may have a freaked-out 'Doctor' and Ford a 'Boss', but only Baldwin/Motion has the machinery. The machinery that *really* makes it. Like the 454 Camaro, the Mean Machine. The machine with more cubes, more horsepower, more suspension, more image and more all-around performance than any other supercar or ponycar on the market. Each one is custom built to order. If bigger cars are your bag, the same hot 454 setups can be had in a Chevelle, Monte Carlo, Nova or even a Street Racer Special. More unbeatables from Baldwin/Motion, the Machinery Makers.

FROM THE MAKERS OF THE FANTASTIC PHASE III GT

THE BALDWIN-MOTION PERFORMANCE GROUP
BALDWIN CHEVROLET/Merrick Road & Central Avenue/Baldwin, L.I., 516-223-7700
MOTION PERFORMANCE, INC./High-Performance Sales-Service Division/598 Sunrise Highway/Baldwin, L.I., N.Y./516-223-3172-3178

When the 454 big-block sent the 427 out to pasture, Baldwin/Motion wasted no time slipping this newest brute under Camaro hoods. Standard "SS-454" equipment included a 454 solid-lifter engine, four-speed transmission, Positraction rear end, Motion heavy-duty suspension, power front disc brakes, a heavy-duty radiator, white-letter tires, bucket seats, chrome valve covers and air cleaner, a 7,500-rpm ignition, and a dyno-tune. The Phase III package added, in addition to the fear of God, "Superbite" traction bars and shocks, an 850-cubic feet per minute , double-pumper carburetor, a high-capacity fuel pump, a special fiberglass hood, special headers, a Phase III ignition, and a SEMA-approved clutch, flywheel, and scattershield. Horsepower on the Phase III factored to about 500 at 6,500 rpm.

Midlife Crisis

For 1974, the Camaro was given its first real face-lift of the new generation. Its nose featured a revised grille opening and the larger, impact-absorbing bumpers required by law. The round taillights used from 1970 to 1973 were replaced by flat, one-piece assemblies. The reworked nose and new bumpers stretched the car's overall length by some 7 inches.

Chevrolet continued to remake the Camaro's identity by shuffling option packages. The Rally Sport option was discontinued for 1974, before being revived a year later. The engine line-up was simplified by the removal of the 307-inch V-8, leaving the 250 six and the 350 V-8 engines as the sole choices. The Z28 was back for 1974 but with the first major alteration of its appearance since 1967. The traditional twin stripes running the length of the car were replaced by huge Z28 graphics on the hood, with three stripes trailing behind each character. The Z28 continued with 245 horsepower, although the engine benefited from the introduction of GM's breakerless High Energy Ignition (HEI). Radial tires also found their way onto the Camaro in 1974.

The end of the 1974 model year saw an unprecedented die-off of musclecars. Sixty-five million years ago the dinosaurs looked up in the sky and surely wondered about that big rock tumbling their way, and so too must American performance enthusiasts have wondered if their day had passed for good. The Plymouth Barracuda and Dodge Challenger were retired, as was the AMC Javelin and AMX. Ford's Mustang II didn't even offer a V-8 in 1974, and for 1975 the 302 was so underpowered Ford may as well not have bothered. The Torino was slowly being transformed into the Ford Elite, which it assuredly was not, and the Cougar was by then a bloated T-Bird clone. Plymouth devalued the Road Runner by affixing its cartoon-inspired stickers to the ho-hum Fury for 1975, and the Dodge Charger was indistinguishable from the lounge-lizard Cordoba. The much-diminished GTO was finally axed, and the Olds 442 was long gone. The Chevelle SS had also long-since departed.

And after 1974, the Z28 Camaro joined them all on a long vacation. Worse, the Z28 wasn't the only exciting Camaro to ride off into the sunset. In 1974 Baldwin/Motion, creator of outrageous 454-powered street-racer Camaros, received a sternly-worded cease-and-desist order from the federal government. Joel Rosen's high-profile engine

The 1972 Z28 was nearly the last Z28, as a prolonged strike at the Ohio assembly plant crippled production at a time when sales were already falling off. On paper the Z was less impressive that year, as net horsepower ratings replaced the old gross ratings used industry-wide. The Z28's power rating was reset at 255. Only 2,575 Z28 Camaros were built in 1972, the lowest total since the option's 1967 introduction. *Roger Huntington Collection/Dobbs Publishing Group*

Chevrolet's new theme for the 1970s was "Building a better way to see the U.S.A." Later Camaro advertising themes de-emphasized performance, as a shrinking performance market and fuel economy concerns took hold.

swaps ran contrary to the government's newly minted emissions regulations, and he was told in no uncertain terms what the penalties would be for continuing the production of his unique Camaros. Defiant to the end, Baldwin/Motion's ads in the early 1970s reminded buyers, "You can still buy real performance!" One of their ads from 1972 showed a 454 Camaro sitting in a graveyard surrounded by the tombstones of the 440 'Cuda, Six-Pack Challenger, 426 Hemi, 429 Mustang, and 429 Cougar.

How could a market that had been so strong less than a decade before whither away so quickly? The reasons were several and long in the making. Escalating insurance rates and "performance surcharges" made many of the cars too expensive for younger people to own. The growing environmental movement had targeted cars as a primary molester of Mother Earth, and a quick look at southern California air quality in the early 1970s made their arguments hard to refute. Plus the early smog controls had de-powered many formerly fast cars and worsened driveability. Many of the cars in this class just weren't as *good* as they used to be. Most had grown too large or were just plain funny looking. These factors all contributed to reduced sales of musclecars, to the point where manufacturers no longer looked upon them as a significant part of the market.

But what truly drove a stake through the heart of the American musclecar was the 1973 Arab oil embargo. Overnight, musclecars became "gas guzzlers," which they had always been, but now the term had a new and sinister meaning. Among the panic legislation the embargo inspired was the federal 55-mile per hour speed limit, which certainly didn't allow for much in the way of exciting driving experiences. Chevrolet wasted little time before playing the good corporate citizen, as Camaro advertising from 1974 encouraged potential customers to "Look and feel good at 55." In this environment, the Z28 was an anachronism and certainly didn't fit in with the new corporate image being constructed by General Motors. The Chevrolet of the future for 1975 was the newly-introduced Monza 2+2, a Vega-based sport coupe powered by four-cylinder V-6 or V-8 engines.

After winning the NHRA Super Stock Eliminator title in 1968, Dave Strickler continued wrestling Camaros down the 1320. Here, he heats the slicks in his early 1970s Pro Stock Camaro. *Courtesy Drag Racing Memories*

There was a ray of high-performance light in the gloom of 1974, however. The Camaro got its own racing series. The International Race of Champions (IROC) had been formed in 1973, pitting the best drivers from all the disciplines of auto racing against each other in identically prepared cars. In that inaugural year the competitors raced Porsche Carreras. Mark Donohue proved as adept behind the wheel of German autobahn rockets as he was behind the wheel of Sunoco-backed American iron and won the first IROC series with three victories in four races. But in 1974, IROC signed on with Chevrolet to run the series with Camaros. The Camaro reign (IROC II) kicked off on September 14 at Michigan International Speedway before continuing on to two races at Riverside and finishing up at Daytona during Speedweek in February 1975. Bobby Unser was the first of the Camaro IROC champions. The IROC Camaro show ran until 1980, when the series went on hiatus, and returned later in the 1980s with an all-new Camaro to wheel about.

With the Z28 retired from duty, the Pontiac Trans-Am became the undisputed performance leader at General Motors in 1975. Even the Corvette had its optional 454-cube V-8 excised that year, leaving the 350 as its largest engine. But with both 400- and 455-inch V-8s still intact, it could be argued that Pontiac's hottest Firebird was the only real American musclecar left. Pontiac produced 27,274 Trans-Ams in 1975, twice the number of Z28s produced in 1974.

What *was* available for Camaro buyers looking for some excitement in 1975 was a revived Rally Sport option. This new Rally Sport's most prominent feature was a flat-black hood, which was appropriate, since there had been a death in the engine room. The top Camaro engine, still the 350 four-barrel, was rated at only 155 horsepower at 3,800 rpm and 250 pounds-feet of torque at 2,400 rpm. The drop was attributed in part to the new catalytic converters introduced on GM cars that year, as the manufacturer fought to keep exhaust emissions low.

An August 1975 *Car and Driver* road test of the Camaro Type LT Rally Sport with 350 V-8 and automatic revealed a quarter mile of 16.8 seconds at 81.5 miles per hour and a top speed of 116 miles per hour—certainly one of the slowest performances turned in by a V-8 Camaro. Still, the Camaro was judged a cut above the rest by *Car and Driver*. "The aging Camaro is the car that continues to make the Monza, enthusiastic little upstart that it is, look foolish," they noted. "The Camaro's days as a street racer are only a memory now, and with the

With its period-correct slotted mags, this Light Copper 1973 Rally Sport is representative of modified Camaros of the 1970s. Slotted mags and a slight rake were musts, and the 350 could be modified a million different ways. The 1973 models were the last to offer the split bumper (the federal bumpers arrived in 1974).

Instead of Chevy Bow Ties, Camaros of the 1970s, like this 1973 model, had their own distinct emblem. Introduced with the 1970 Camaro, the emblem was used throughout the decade and into the early 1980s.

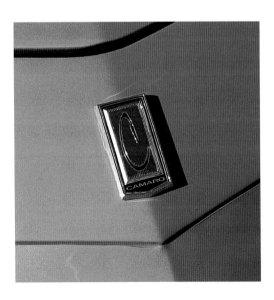

350-cubic inch two- and four-barrel V-8s the only engines available besides the six, the car has settled into senescence as a boulevardier who no longer has any intention of getting his new suit messed up in a one-on-one scuffle . . . What remains the Camaro's strong suit is the one thing legislation is hard pressed to take away from it: handling."

The Camaro's handling ability was spiced up with the new, optional Z86 gymkhana suspension, priced at a reasonable $112, or $66 when ordered with Type LT or Rally Sport Camaros. It included upgraded shocks, steering gear, and rear stabilizer bar, 15x7-inch wheels, and E60-15 tires. One improvement introduced in 1975 was the wrap-around rear glass, which helped eliminate a traditional F-car blind spot. Additionally, power door locks joined the option list, a $56 feature. The Camaro may have been getting slower, but it at least was turning into a more comfortable car, suitable for long-distance touring.

Little was changed on the Camaro for 1976. A mid-range V-8 was again available though, with the introduction of the 305-inch small-block. It became the standard engine on the Type LT. Fed through a two-barrel Rochester carburetor, it was rated at 140 horsepower at 3,800 rpm and 245 pounds-feet of torque at 2,000 rpm. Interestingly, it could be teamed with the performance rear axle and four-speed transmission (except in California). The top engine remained the LM1 350 four-barrel, rated at 165 horsepower. Cruise control was added to the option list, and another of the 1970's fads, the half-vinyl roof, was optional. The styling of the Type LT model was altered slightly, with an aluminum panel mounted between the taillights. A windshield-type antenna was included with the various radio options.

By 1976, many at Chevrolet were nursing second thoughts about putting the Z28 to sleep. Trans-Am production had reached 46,701 cars in 1976, and Camaro sales were improving. Clearly there was still a market for performance cars. Additionally, the public had had time to digest the increased price of gasoline.

With all indicators pointing back toward fun, Chevrolet announced midway through the 1977 model year that the Z28 would return. Chevrolet general manager Bob Lund made the announcement January 14, 1977, at a Daytona press conference. This time Chevrolet had no qualms about touting the car's heritage. "You remember this car. Low and lean. Born to run. It's back. The Z28," ads promised. And instead of an option package, this time the Z28 was a separate model, priced at $5,170.

Appearance-wise, the 1977 Z28 was unlike earlier editions. The twin stripes were gone, but the car stood out thanks to body-color bumpers and wheels, a blacked-out grille with Z28 emblem, sport mirrors, large Z28 graphics on the fenders, an unusual teardrop decal on the hood, and front and rear spoilers.

Functionally, the standard Z28 boasted a modified F41 suspension, heavy-duty Borg-Warner four-speed, a quicker 14:1 steering ratio, and the 350 four-barrel V-8, with rumblier dual-resonator exhaust, rated at 170 horsepower. Performance was helped considerably by steep axle ratios of 3.42:1 for automatics and 3.73:1 for four-speeds.

Car Craft magazine, in an August 1977 test of an L-82 Corvette, Monza Spyder, and the 1977 Z28 with four-speed and 3.73 rear axle, netted a 15.21 quarter mile at 91.34 miles per hour in the Z28. The Corvette was good for a 15.07, the Monza a 16.90. *Car Craft* editors were pleasantly surprised. "The L48 powerplant felt considerably stronger than we had expected, considering that it's 40 horsepower shy of the L82 350-cubic inch [Corvette] engine," they wrote. "Banging gears at Irwindale brought back the old feeling—the Hurst linkage was so smooth and fairly begged to be powershifted." Unfortunately, Californians could not experience that "old feeling" with the Hurst shifter, as the Z28

Although rarely ordered, the 350-cubic inch two-barrel V-8 could be teamed with a four-speed transmission. The four-speed tranny was a $200 option.

The 1975 Camaros were given a wraparound rear window that helped open up the second-generation car's blind spot and "Unleaded fuel only" stickers to go with the new catalytic converter. With no Z28 or SS model to carry the flag, the 1975 Camaros are remembered (or forgotten) as having one of the weakest V-8 engine line-ups in Camaro history. Shown is the Type LT model. *Detroit Public Library National Automotive History Collection*

with manual transmission couldn't pass the state's stringent emissions regulations.

Still, it was good just to have the Z28 back. "Surprisingly, in this age of low-performance smog motors, the car's major problem was traction," *Car Craft* noted. "A 3.73 cog in the rear axle housing really put the power to the pavement. Side-stepping the clutch produced voluminous clouds of smoke and less-than satisfactory time slips."

1977 Z28 Breakdown

When the Z28 returned to the Camaro line-up early in 1977, it was sold not as an option package but as a separate model, with prices starting at $5,170. Like many of the 1970's musclecars, it relied heavily on tape stripes for visual appeal. Chevrolet even considered a Trans-Am-like, flaming Z28 hood decal but fortunately restrained itself. Although the solid-lifter cam of years past was long gone, the Z28's spec sheet revealed an impressive list of hardware, especially for the times.

Camaro Z28 equipment included:
- 350-ci, 170-hp V-8
- Heavy-duty Borg-Warner 4-speed transmission
- Dual resonator exhaust
- 14:1 steering ratio
- F-41 sport suspension
- Front and rear stabilizer bars
- Body-colored 15x7 wheels
- White-letter GR70 radials
- Body-colored bumpers
- Front and rear spoilers
- Z28 graphics on hood, grille, and fenders

Other testers were impressed with the Z28's handling abilities.

After a two-year-plus absence from the 1970s musclecar scene, Chevrolet's Z28 had some ground to make up. Due to the late introduction, Chevrolet built only 14,349 Z28s for 1977, compared to 68,744 Pontiac Trans-Ams. But the return of the Z28 created a bubble of excitement around the Camaro, helping push production over 200,000 cars for the first time since 1969. The Mustang didn't come close. The old friend was back, and the public approved.

A Final Makeover

In 1978, the Camaro was given some plastic surgery, the better to keep the aging body style fresh. The exposed bumpers went away, replaced by body-colored endcaps that hid the actual bumpers. The taillamps were redesigned as well. T-tops were introduced as a $625 option. A good idea on paper, especially during a time when convertibles were virtually extinct, the F-body T-tops suffered in their execution. They tended to leak, and thieves quickly discovered the tinted-glass roof panels were easy to steal.

The Z28 was given a more aggressive appearance for 1978. New additions included fender louvers and a fake hood scoop that traced the hood decal's lines. "His majesty," as Chevrolet advertising copywriters called the Z28, now sported 185 horsepower, except in California. Again, Californians were a shiftless lot, only able to purchase Z28s with automatic transmissions.

The Rally Sport option ceased and became a separate model, and its features were spread throughout the Camaro line. There was a Rally Sport Coupe and a Type LT Rally Sport Coupe, in addition to the standard Sport Coupe, Type LT Coupe, and Z28. Not surprisingly, the Z28 was the most expensive of the lot at $5,603.

These changes and a strong economy made a tremendous year for Camaro. The 272,631 production run was a new Camaro record and has only been exceeded once since. Z28 production reached 54,907, also a new record, although the Trans-Am still ruled the segment with production of 93,341. During the 1978 model year Chevrolet also built the two-millionth Camaro, a significant milestone for a car that was nearly canceled only six years earlier.

But the upside of the roller coaster wasn't finished yet, as the 1979 models turned out to be the best-selling Camaros in history. Production hit an amazing 282,571,

while the Z28 was also the most popular in Camaro history up to that time with 84,877 produced. Firebird sales were huge again, this despite the fact Ford had just introduced a capable new Mustang.

The 1979 Camaro was not substantially different from the previous years' offerings, but there were a few new attractions. The Berlinetta model was introduced, taking the place in the line-up formerly held by the Type LT. As the new luxury Camaro, the Berlinetta offered extra insulation, a distinct grille and pinstriping, bright moldings around the windows, and a suspension tuned for a plush ride. A redesigned instrument panel helped freshen the Camaro's interior, while upgrades such as a power antenna and stereo cassette player helped modernize the car.

For the Z28, Chevy ads emphasized handling. "When it comes to hugging the road, there's nothing quite like the feel of a Camaro Z28. It's the hugger's hugger," the ads claimed. Externally, the Z28 got its annual striping revision plus a new front air dam. The Z28's LM1 350 was rated at 175 horsepower in 49-state tune, or 170 horsepower in California. Z28 prices started at $6,115.35. Standard equipment included the 350 four-barrel, four-speed transmission, simulated

bolt-on hood scoop with black throat, blacked-out window and windshield moldings, two-tone striping, fender louvers, front and rear spoilers, blacked-out grille, black headlamp- and taillamp-bezels, black-out rear panel, body-colored sport mirrors, door handle inserts and back bumper, and white-letter P225/70R15 radials on body color 7-inch-wide wheels.

The 1980 Z28 got the usual new stripes along its flanks plus half-flares at the rear wheel openings. A new grille with a revised cross-hatch pattern made its debut. But one functional change seemed inspired by the Chevys of the 1960s. The Z28 offered a rear-facing hood scoop with solenoid-operated flaps that let in a blast of cold air to the 190-horsepower, 350 V-8. Every little bit helped, but at 3,660 pounds, the Z28 was good for about 14 miles per gallon, and in 1980, that was the sort of thing people really noticed.

Car and Driver conducted a road test of the 1980 Z28 and clocked a quarter mile of 16.4 seconds at 86 miles per hour. In its report, as in much of the media, there was plenty of doom and gloom about the future of thirsty V-8 American musclecars, especially after the Iranian revolution sent fuel prices skyrocketing once again. The magazine's general assessment of the aging Z28

The last of the Z28s (for a while, anyway), the 1974 edition sported the type of large hood graphics that would infect much of America's performance car line-up in the 1970s. Although not quite the race-car-in-street clothing the earlier Z28s were, the Z28 option still cost only $572. Chevrolet built 13,802 Z28s for 1974. *Detroit Public Library National Automotive History Collection*

was not pretty. "The Z28, before our very eyes, has become a museum piece. The transformation required only a few years, but it is complete. Henceforth, you will find the Z28 cataloged under the heading 'Warfare, Medieval.' Its subheading is 'Armor, personal,'" they wrote. "And, just as medieval jousting was phased out in the face of more modern methods of aggression, cars like the Z28 are folding beneath the pressure of more modern methods of combining excitement and transportation. The time has come when it is only right that cars such as the Z28 should metamorphose."

Museum piece or no, the Z28 was nonetheless one of the few cars of the era

IROC Camaros mix it up at Riverside in October 1975. Shown is Benny Parsons leading Richard Petty. The IROC racers ran back-to-back events on October 25 and 26 at Riverside in 1975 during the four-race IROC III season, with Bobby Unser taking the first race and Bobby Allison the second. High finishes helped A. J. Foyt win the series title that season despite not winning any of the races. *Bob Tronolone*

that still offered a V-8 and manual transmission. The 1980 Mustang had a 255-cubic inch V-8 and automatic transmission as its most potent combination, with a twitchy 2.3-liter, turbo four-cylinder as the only performance option. The once-mighty Trans-Am offered only one engine, a turbocharged, 210-horsepower, 301-cubic inch V-8 mated to an automatic transmission.

Chevrolet's work on improving the Camaro's fuel economy, though, was more evident with the base Sport Coupe and Rally Sport models. A 267-cubic inch (4.4-liter) small-block V-8—rated at 120 horsepower—took its place below the 305 for 1980. The 250-inch straight six was finally retired and replaced by two fuel-efficient, 3.8-liter V-6s—one a 229-cubic inch engine built by Chevrolet, the other the 231 V-6 built by Buick. It marked the first time a non-Chevrolet engine was available in the Camaro. California Z28s

were also a bit more economical, as they were limited to the 305-inch V-8.

Sales were not good for either the Camaro or Firebird in 1980, as the economy settled into a recession and high interest rates discouraged many potential buyers from signing up. The second oil crisis, stemming from the revolution in oil-producing Iran, continued into the early 1980s, wrecking sales for the 1981 Camaro, as well. Only 43,272 Z28s were produced out of 126,139 Camaros total, the lowest number since 1973. One reason was a huge inflation-driven price increase. Z28 prices jumped nearly $900 from 1980 to 1981, cresting the $8,000 mark for the first time. The Camaro line-up was further streamlined by the removal of the Rally Sport model, once again. At least California buyers got some good news, as they could once again purchase a Camaro with a V-8

The 1979 Camaro was the most popular ever, with 282,571 produced. New styling touches that year for the Z28 included the front fender vents and wraparound front spoiler. The striping scheme is also unique to that year's Z28, as Chevrolet changed the performance model's trim yearly during the late 1970s. Z28 production hit a whopping 84,877 in 1979 and was the last great year before the second energy crisis hit. *Detroit Public Library National Automotive History Collection*

and a four-speed transmission, even if it was only the 305.

Other efficiency improvements came from teaming most engine combinations with higher gear ratios and the introduction of Chevy's Advanced Computer Command Control engine-management system. Computer-controlled lock-up torque converters helped automatic transmission cars save a few sips of fuel.

Ads urged buyers to, "Spread Your Wings. The new Z28 is for anyone who wants to move up from automotive tedium. It's for those rare drivers who understand the rush of the road and the thrust of finely machined road cars. That's the way it's always been." Maybe, but more and more buyers were spreading their wings and flapping on over to the Toyota or Honda dealership. Whereas at the beginning of the second-generation Camaro's life it was considered daring and fast, increasingly people just viewed the Camaro as an old, creaky gas hog.

Ironically, just as the Camaro was about to be revamped for the coming decade, an old name from the car's muscular past reasserted itself. Yenko Chevrolet, creator of the wonderful 427-powered Yenko sYc Camaros in the late 1960s, took another shot at building monster Camaros in 1981 with its Yenko Turbo-Z. Conceived in late 1979, with 1980 spent on research and development, the Yenko Turbo-Z relied on tur-

bocharging technology to find the lost horsepower, while still passing the sniff test. This time, Yenko had to be certified as a small manufacturer to get his creations built.

The logic was explained in Yenko's promotional literature. "From a performance standpoint, cars have shown a slow but steady decline in the last 10 years. Low compression engines to accommodate low octane fuel are now the norm," the sales pitch read. "Ever increasing numbers of emission controls have sapped their share of horsepower from once potent engines. To recover these accumulated power losses without increasing pollution presents a real challenge."

Yenko's solution was a Turbo International turbo system. "Our system uses no priority valve, so there's no turbo-lag. We don't have a waste gate to malfunction either. And since all of the fuel entering the engine is processed through the turbo, you get better economy and improved response even without being in boost," the promotional material explained. "This has all been developed with each and every emission control connected and functional."

The 1981 Yenko Turbo-Z Stage 1 Camaro had a base price of $11,300, which included the turbocharger, automatic transmission, Stage I wheels, and Turbo-Z graphics. It was available in six colors. The sultans in the audience could have the Yenko Turbo-Z Stage II, with a base price of $17,500.

It included adjustable leather seats, a competition steering wheel covered in leather, Koni shocks, modified stabilizer bars, and modular wheels with Goodyear Wingfoot tires. Few Yenko Turbo-Zs were built, but it was good that old-style power levels were available off a showroom floor, even if the price was not for the average hot rodder.

The 1981 Camaro was widely known to be a lame duck, with next generation 1982 Camaros popping up in spy photos and news accounts everywhere. Cars like the 280 ZX turbo, Toyota Supra, and Mazda RX-7 were capturing larger shares of affluent young buyers. The second-generation Camaro had survived an entire decade with essentially the same sheet metal and mechanicals under the skin, no mean feat in an era where the American automotive market was turned upside-down. But with a second fuel crisis still fresh on the minds of consumers and increasing regulation out of Washington in the form of Corporate Average Fuel Economy (CAFE) standards and tightening emission controls, clearly a new type of Camaro was needed. Smaller, lighter, and cleaner were the new buzzwords for all cars, and the upcoming Camaro would be all of those.

The last of the second-generation Camaros, the 1981 models sold at less than half the pace they had only two years earlier. The twin scourges for the Camaro were economic recession and high fuel prices, although after 12 years with the same basic body, the public could be forgiven for being bored. Z28 production was 43,272. *Detroit Public Library National Automotive History Collection*

5

Chapter
Five

The Tortoise Becomes the Hare:
1982–1992

S ay what you will about the 1982 Camaro (and there were plenty of opinions about its performance and quality control), but on one aspect of the car most people agree: the 1982 Camaro was just flat gorgeous. Much like the 1970 Camaro had done upon its introduction, when the 1982 version debuted in late 1981, it instantly made every other American sport coupe look old and ugly. The car was sleeker, and the Z28 was less-gaudily striped than the car it replaced. As a bonus, the new Camaro's handling abilities left its competitors wallowing in its wake. The 1982 Z28 even helped kick off the performance wars of the 1980s, although that was not apparent at the time.

That's a pretty good resume for a car that nearly arrived to market in radically different form. Designing the next-generation Camaro during the late 1970s, a fuel-conscious era when the future of V-8-powered automobiles was itself in doubt, spawned much debate over what shape and mechanical layout the Camaro should take. There was talk of economical front-wheel-drive Camaros, mid-engine Camaros, future Z28s without V-8s—and a few traditionalists who were holding out for a continuation of the successful V-8, rear-wheel-drive formula.

Fortunately, the traditionalists won out. It's pure speculation, but a front-wheel-drive Camaro spun off the upcoming X-car platform would likely have been a disaster, a watered-down pretender, a grim reminder of better times. For proof, note the entrance and quick exit of the Beretta GTZ, Lumina Z34, Cavalier Z24, and every other front-wheel-drive performance coupe Chevrolet has tried to sell since the early 1980s. There may have been differing ideas within General Motors, but on the street the precedent

had already been set: real Camaros have V-8 engines and rear-wheel drive.

They also have exciting styling, and Bill Porter's Advanced Design Studio started the development of design themes that would eventually morph into the 1982 Camaro. The final shape crystallized after Chevrolet Design Chief Jerry Palmer led an intense competition against the Pontiac studio led by John Schinella for F-Car final design. A little of both division's influence ended up in the final product, and both managed to create a distinctive look for their own respective F-cars. It wasn't all just looks, either: the drag coefficient for the 1982 Camaro was a slippery .37, with the Firebird posting even better numbers thanks to hidden headlamps.

For the interior, similarly bold concepts were being suggested, although the final product was perhaps less successful than the exterior. The aircraft-inspired dashboard was flat and deeply hooded, with control pods jutting from either side of the instrument binnacle. Packaging considerations left no room for a glove compartment, but there was a large space carved out for front-seat passengers. Quirky features like a dual-face speedometer, reading to both 85 miles per hour and 140 kilometers per hour, helped contribute to the Camaro's unique personality, as did the large eight-ball shifter.

The armrests on the doors swept upward to panels containing the door handles and locks. The speedometer and tach held down the outboard positions on the dash, while quarter-sized fuel, temperature, and voltmeter gauges were crowded in between. The look of the interior was very sharp and angular, with few curves—all parts looked either crisply folded or pulled tight over surfaces. It almost looked as if you might cut

With a lower price than the Z28, the RS convertible proved the more popular of the two droptop Camaros for 1992. The 1992 Camaros were given 25th anniversary emblems on the dash and could be ordered with a special Heritage Package. *Chevrolet*

yourself on some of the interior pieces if you weren't careful.

But looks and features aside, the 1982 Camaro was functionally better too, at least in most ways. Tom Zimmer, chief Camaro engineer starting in 1976, worked his enthusiastic team hard to update the Camaro for the coming decade. The new Camaro was smaller and lighter than the 1981 models, with a wheelbase 7 inches stubbier and an overall length that measured 10 inches shorter. The new car was 2 inches narrower, and the overall height was a fraction less. Interior room was approximately the same, pulled out a little here, pushed in a little there. Curb weight was roughly 250 pounds less.

Additionally, there were major improvements in chassis stiffness, thanks to a completely unitized body. Underneath, the vintage suspension configuration used since 1967 was tossed out in favor of modified MacPherson front struts and a torque-arm rear suspension. The switch to the compact MacPherson strut design allowed a lower hoodline, among other advantages, while the long torque-arm design for the rear suspension eliminated any traces of power hop.

From the beginning, the Z28's favored place in the product line was factored into the engineering mix. Camaros ordered with the F41 suspension and the Z28 were given responsive recirculating ball steering, while base models made do with worm-and-sector steering. The Z28 had a fast 14.0:1 steering ratio and could be ordered with four-wheel disc brakes for $179 extra. The standard

Z28 tires were P215/65R15s mounted on unique aluminum rims.

With all that was new it was easy to be dazzled, but the 1982 Camaro had a few handicaps. One drawback was the Camaro's choice of three-speed automatic or four-speed manual transmissions at a time when most of the world was shifting to four-speed automatics and five-speed manuals. Even the cheapest economy cars of the time offered more up-to-date transmission offerings than the 1982 Camaro.

The other handicap was much more serious. Basically, the new Z28 was seeking glory without any guts. The car was widely ridiculed for being underpowered—a car that looked so fast shouldn't have been so slow. The base Z28 engine was the 305-cubic inch V-8 with four-barrel carburetor, rated at 145 horsepower at 4,000 rpm and 240 pounds-feet of torque at 2,400 rpm. It was available with either four-speed manual transmission or automatic. There was one engine option that, while being visually impressive, didn't offer much more in the way of speed.

For $450 extra, buyers could select the 305 V-8 topped with a unique twin-throttle-body fuel-injection setup. The "Cross-Fire Injection" system featured twin-throttle bodies on a cross-ram manifold. With the injection system, the 305 was rated at 165 horsepower at 4,200 rpm and 240 pounds-feet of torque at 2,400 rpm, a slight improvement. The twin-throttle-body system was only available with the automatic transmission, though, as the TBI/four-speed combo failed to elude the federal gas-guzzler

With the 1982 Camaro, the Z28 was the target model and not an afterthought. Incredible road-holding ability was the third-generation Camaro's specialty, if at the cost of a harsh ride. *Detroit Public Library National Automotive History Collection*

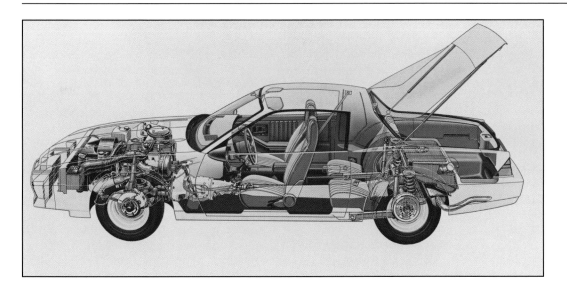

This cutaway shows the new features of the 1982 Camaro, including the MacPherson strut front suspension, torque-arm rear suspension, and curved-glass hatch. As illustrated here, the 1982 Camaros had the dubious distinction of being the first to have a four-cylinder engine underhood. The 151-cubic inch (2.5-liter) Pontiac four produced 90 horsepower at 4,000 rpm and 132 pounds-feet of torque at 2,800 rpm—the lowest power rating in any Camaro. The four-cylinder was offered from 1982 to 1986. *Roger Huntington Collection/Dobbs Publishing Group*

classification of the time. The Cross-Fire system also failed the California sniff test and was not available for sale there.

Car and Driver magazine tested a 1982 Z28 with the 165-horsepower TBI engine and recorded a 16.0-second quarter mile at 85 miles per hour. Top speed was 116 miles per hour. They were not impressed. "And its engine room is a disaster area," Don Sherman wrote. "It matters little which array of four, six, or eight cylinders you match up with your choice of carburetion or fuel injection, nor will a stern insistence on a shift-it-yourself transmission make much difference. When the stoplight turns green and accelerators snap to the floor, the Z28 is Emily Post polite: everybody else goes first."

Later in the year, *Car and Driver* put together the expected Camaro versus Firebird versus Mustang GT showdown, with a twist—a Porsche 928 was thrown into the mix. Their quarter-mile time for the throttle-body Z28 was even slower, at 16.4 seconds. They found that even though the Camaro had more horsepower than the Mustang (the 1982 Mustang GT offered 157 horsepower), the Camaro's 3,400-pound curb weight and lack of a manual transmission put it at a disadvantage. The Mustang's ET was 16.2 seconds at 86 miles per hour.

As expected, where the Z28 excelled was in the handling comparison. "When you drive a Z28, there is one engineering breakthrough that slaps you right in the face: this Camaro is not a committee car. The shock valving is so tight that you feel pebbles on the pavement as you back out of a parking space. And the steering response in uncannily import-like to the touch," they wrote.

The writers circled the skid pad at .81 g in the Z28, equaling the Porsche's best.

Road & Track also praised the 1982 Camaro's handling prowess. "Whereas the old Z28 would bounce sideways at the mere hint of a bump while cornering, it takes a rougher stretch of pavement to upset the new one's poise," they noted.

Motor Trend magazine was a bit more charitable to the new Camaro, naming the Z28 its Car of the Year. The editors tested a four-barrel/four-speed car for their May 1982 issue and recorded a 16.67 quarter mile at 81 miles per hour, also slower than the Mustang GT tested in the same issue. "But as a total package, considering roadworthiness, visual appeal, and design derring-do, the Camaro undebatably represents a superior job," they judged. "The difference is a matter of extra effort. You see it in the extensive chassis reinforcement that minimizes front end deflection to sharpen steering response. You see it in the serious suspension calibration and tire choice that yield skid-pad test numbers in a league with vastly more expensive exoticars. You see it in sleek and aerodynamic sheet metal that is incapable of going unnoticed. You *don't* see it, at the moment, in the engine/transmission team we tested, but that just leaves the engineers something to keep them busy."

As a final honor, the 1982 Z28 was named the Indy 500 Pace Car, the third time the Z28 received that honor. Jim Rathmann, the 1960 Indy 500 race winner who had also piloted the 1969 Camaro Pace Car, was chosen to drive the new edition. Chevrolet wasted little time selling the new Pace Car as a collectible. "Now you can own a street version of this special Z28 Camaro in an edition so limited that only one will be offered to each American Chevrolet dealership," ads read. Instead of being an option package, the Z50 Indy Edition was a separate model offered in addition to the base Sport Coupe, Berlinetta, and Z28. The 1982 Pace Cars were all silver with blue and red accent striping and Sixty-Sixth Indianapolis 500 logos. The blue and silver color scheme carried over into the cloth and vinyl interior. Underhood, both versions of the 305 V-8 were available. The Pace Car sold for $900 more than a base Z28.

By most measuring sticks, the new Camaro was a fabulous success. Production increased more than 60,000 over the 1981 edition, and looks and handling abilities reached new heights. But after the shine wore off the new Camaro, problems became apparent. Many buyers reported disturbing reliability problems for the early third-generation cars: from minor irritations like wheel center-caps that perpetually fell off, to potentially more serious problems like water that collected in the Cross-Fire V-8's air cleaner, forcing a recall. General Motors clearly still had a way to go in smoothly incorporating government-required safety and emissions technologies and reaching Japanese levels of quality control.

With all that was new it was easy to be dazzled, but the 1982 Camaros are also interesting for being true transitional cars between the 1970s and 1980s. While 1982 Z28s were the first to offer fuel injection

(such as it was), they were also the last year in which an 8-track tape player could be ordered in a Camaro. They were still powered by the small-block Chevy V-8, yet they were the first Camaros to be smaller and lighter than their predecessors and the first to offer a four-cylinder engine underhood, the better to combat anticipated future energy crises. And while the 1982 Camaro only produced 1970s-era horsepower levels, the pieces were in place for a much stronger Z28 later in the 1980s.

More Power

The universal criticism of the 1982 Z28 was its lack of power, but of all the possible deficiencies a Camaro could have, that was probably the easiest to fix. Yes, federal regulations were tighter than they had been, but small-block Chevy V-8s still responded to the same tweaks they always had, and there was no shortage of engineering talent at Chevrolet that knew how to make them run. Sure enough, a fix arrived in mid-1983, and that fix relied on time-tested Chevrolet hot-rodding techniques.

Labeled the 5.0 H.O., the L69 305 produced 190 horsepower at 4,800 rpm and 240 pounds-feet of torque at 3,200 rpm. The H.O. developed the extra power thanks to a Corvette-spec cam and catalyst plus larger exhaust pipes. Chevrolet dumped the Cross-Fire fuel injection for a Rochester four-barrel carburetor on the H.O. (although the Cross-Fire setup was still available, rated at 175 horsepower in 1983) and opened up the breathing with a dual-snorkel air cleaner. Chevrolet addressed the other criticism leveled against the Camaro's powertrain with the introduction of a Borg-Warner T-5 five-speed transmission.

The 5.0 H.O. and five-speed transformed the Camaro and removed the largest criticism against the car. The engine sounded tough, revved quickly, and just *felt* good. The Firebird also shared in this bounty, which was a good thing since Ford had just installed a Holley four-barrel atop its own 5.0-liter H.O., bringing the Mustang GT's horsepower up to 175. Other rumblings of a performance war for the 1980s were also starting to be heard. Carroll Shelby had recently teamed with Chrysler in an attempt to recreate some old magic, and the 1983 Shelby Charger was the first product of their union. It wasn't much, really, just a four-cylinder hatchback with fat tires, loud stripes, and a mild horsepower increase, but it hinted of future projects

still to come. The 5.0 H.O. Z28 put the Camaro at the front of this race.

The difference between the 1982 and 1983 Z28 could be measured immediately. *Motor Trend* recorded a quarter mile of 15.55 at 90.5 miles per hour in an H.O. Camaro. *Car and Driver* editors, ever the hotshoes, pounded out a 15.0 at 93 miles per hour with the new engine package for their June 1983 issue, besting a 1983 Mustang GT's 15.4 at 90 miles per hour. Top speed was up substantially over the Cross-Fire 1982 Z28 to 134 miles per hour. They liked the extra power but still cited the superior handling and stability of the Z28 as the car's best talent. "If you like low-speed stunt driving accompanied by clouds of tire smoke, the Mustang GT gets it. But when it comes to real driving, to harnessing the power of a big American V-8 and putting it down on the road, the Camaro Z28 H.O. is the clear winner," they wrote.

It was in 1983 that the Camaro became a clear winner on the race track again, too. The dueling Camaros of David Hobbs and Willy T. Ribbs traded victories throughout the entire 1983 SCCA Trans-Am schedule, with Hobbs finally winning out, 158 points to 148. Although Ribbs scored five wins to Hobbs' four that year, Ribbs had to overcome poor finishes at Summit Point, Seattle, and Road America. A Camaro Z28 also won the 24-hour Longest Day at Nelson Ledges race in 1983.

With the 1984 Camaro came further refinement, thanks to a slightly revised suspension. Accolades continued to flow for the Z28. It won a best-handling American car contest at *Car and Driver*, defeating Chevy's own Corvette, the Pontiac Fiero, Mustang SVO, and Dodge Daytona Turbo Z. The Z28 pulled a .81 g in the road-holding test and handled the street tests with considerable poise. "Unlike the Corvette, the Z28 encourages its driver to explore the upper registers, and its chassis sends back honest assessments of the situation at hand," they noted. "Steaming into the tight turns of our serpentine road course through the San Gabriel Mountains brought on a smidgen of understeer. A lift of the right foot, and the tail would nudge out proportionately, though it was easy to check with the proper amount of opposite steering lock."

With an improving economy, good sales figures for the Camaro, and the budding performance war against Ford's Mustang GT continuing to build, Chevrolet even took the unusual step of including a quarter-mile ET in its print ads. "This is the best time we've ever had," the ad bragged. Listed with the car's technical specifications was a 0–60 mile per hour time of 7.2 seconds and a quarter-mile elapsed time of 15.2 seconds.

The other news for 1984 was a revised Berlinetta model heavy on techno flash and futuristic gewgaws. This new Berlinetta interior was typical of 1980s attempts to reinvent the instrument panel using flashing lights and digital readouts in place of sweeping needles on numbered backgrounds. The Berlinetta was given electronic readouts for everything, including the tach. An overhead console provided more digital data, and a unique upright cassette stereo was affixed to the console, mounted to swivel for either driver and passenger use. "Welcome aboard Starship Camaro," the ads encouraged, showing the twinkling dash, with a view of the solar system through the windshield. "Camaro Berlinetta. Climb in. Buckle up. Adjust the retractable, touch-sensitive instrument pods so your hands never have to leave the wheel to control vital functions. Turn the key and watch the system monitor perform seven preflight tests as the engine sparks to life. Blip the throttle and watch the vacuum-fluorescent display and optional graphic equalizer. Now, put it in gear, give it

some gas, and watch the digital speedometer numbers multiply. Your journey has begun."

For all the Star-Trek hyperbole, it was a somewhat less than successful execution, unnecessarily complex and expensive. For the first time, the Berlinetta was actually more expensive than the Z28.

Smoothing the Bumps

While performance was rapidly improving on the Camaro, Chevrolet was working steadily behind the scenes to meet the latest round of regulations and smooth some of the car's rough edges. Chuck Hughes, who had earlier worked as a development engineer at the Milford proving grounds when the Camaro was new, was named chief engineer at Camaro and Firebird in 1985, holding the position until 1988.

Improving the Camaro's reliability was a major focus of his tenure. "Every chief in Chevy was working on improved reliability and customer satisfaction," he recalled. "I'm not sure exactly where Camaro was at that time, but Honda and Toyota were really setting the pace out there. I think they [Honda and Toyota] were running at two problems per vehicle, and probably the industry was running at four or five on an average. Those are things you have to go to the dealer for in

The IROC-Z28 debuted in 1985, as Chevrolet attempted to get more mileage out of its association with the all-star International Race of Champions. The IROC was initially an option package for the Z28 (it was later a separate model) that included 16-inch aluminum wheels, special suspensions front and rear, a larger stabilizer bar, Delco/Bilstein shocks, and a front frame reinforcement. *Roger Huntington Collection/ Dobbs Publishing Group*

the first 12,000 miles." At least half of the efforts of Hughes' department was devoted to "cleaning up" reliability problems. "We applied great pressure to the marketing groups to keep changes under control, so it didn't consume our engineers' time," he said.

Hughes also believed the Camaros and Firebirds delivered poor ride quality: "It was pretty bone-jarring, and unnecessarily so." It became a priority to make the cars "handle well and still get the good impact isolation." According to Hughes, "[The] development group spent a considerable amount of time on getting that under control and still being able to retain wheel control and good cornering in sport terms."

Hughes' staff worked hard to improve the handling characteristics associated with the solid rear axle, refining the system to the point where it nearly equaled the performance of an expensive independent rear suspension setup. By the time Hughes' team was through, every suspension part had been scrutinized. "The initial part of it was Bilstein shocks," Hughes said. "Then later, Delco came in with their own deflected-disc shocks, which performed even better than the Bilsteins at considerably less money. There was a transition there, of Bilsteins doing the job, and then later deflected-disc Delco shocks that were even better."

Other improvements came through massaging the Camaro's caster settings. "We didn't have enough caster in the car. With the strut suspension, increasing the caster means moving the towers quite a ways . . . We were shooting for 4 1/4 degrees of caster. We actually wound up retooling the tower," Hughes recalled. "When you have a strut front suspension, it has some advantages, but one thing it doesn't have is a good camber-change curve . . . . And so you go to a lot of subtleties to compensate for that."

The first Camaro to benefit from more sophisticated underpinnings was the IROC Camaro introduced in 1985. The $659 IROC option included revised Delco front struts, unique jounce bumpers, Bilstein gas shocks in the rear, a larger 24-millimeter rear stabilizer bar, a slightly lower ride height, and P245/50VR16 Goodyear Eagle Gatorback tires.

The L69 305 H.O. V-8 was standard equipment with the IROC, but lurking on the option list was the successor to the short-lived Cross-Fire fuel-injected V-8. The LB9 305 V-8 with Tuned Port Injection (TPI) was introduced that year, available only with four-speed automatic transmission and rated

at 215 horsepower. The TPI system was a much more sophisticated electronic-port fuel-injection setup, with a manifold that featured long, curved individual intake runners to promote good torque characteristics. The TPI used a mass air flow sensor to measure incoming air. Thanks to the fuel injection's greater efficiency, the TPI's power increase came with no fuel mileage penalty—in fact, fuel economy increased slightly.

Popular Hot Rodding magazine found the TPI/automatic combination good for a 15.45 quarter mile at 89.5 miles per hour in its April 1985 issue, but the writers had a few reservations. They observed the TPI 305 ran out of steam at 4,000 rpm, although at full throttle the transmission tended to shift at 5,000 rpm. "As we had surmised, the Camaro's automatic transmission proved to be its downfall. Although our drivers could load the converter for a good start, the engine refused to shift prior to the 5,000-rpm mark unless the driver lifted from the accelerator, a maneuver which also succeeded in hurting the car's elapsed time," The 210-horsepower Mustang GT they tested at the same time ran a 14.89 quarter mile, while a four-cylinder Shelby Charger turbo nearly equaled the Camaro with a 15.83 ET. The Z28 still ruled the skid pad though, with .823-g performance.

Motor Trend also tested the TPI 305, running a 15.30 at 89 miles per hour. "The extra torque of the TPI system was quite noticeable, especially exiting the various slow corners at Mid-Ohio," they wrote. "The L69 version, of course, had the five-speed manual transmission, but the TPI with automatic was marginally faster because of the superior power and response characteristics of the injected engine." Also benefiting from the blessing of multi-port fuel injection was the 2.8-liter V-6, which jumped to 135 horsepower with the change.

In the early 1980s, Z28s were no terror at the drag strip, but they were great for grassroots autocrossing. It was one arena where a Z28 driver could be assured of smoking a Mustang. The Camaro's T-top option was not cheap, costing roughly $800 at the time, but that was as close to a convertible as a Camaro buyer could get (and it opened up room for a racing helmet, as this driver discovered).

Besides the powertrain upgrades, the Camaro enjoyed the first body modifications of the new generation in 1985. The Z28 and IROC received a slightly altered front fascia, revised rocker-panel skirts, and louvered hood inserts. The Camaro's available palette of colors was almost completely revised for 1985, with some bright new hues getting a try-out. The alterations continued for 1986 as more nanny-state regulations assumed their place in the federal register, the most prominent being the center-high-mount stoplight (CHMSL), or third brake light as it is commonly known on the street.

That year the last hold-over pieces from the 1970s disappeared in the Camaro. It was the last year for a four-speed manual transmission in a Camaro and the last year for the Berlinetta, which was canceled early in the year after only 4,479 were built. Chevrolet toughened up the lower-end models this year by making the F41 sport suspension standard equipment across the board. Camaros with the V-6 got the sport suspension with P215/65R15 blackwall tires on 15x7-inch styled steel wheels and a sport tone exhaust. Four-cylinder Camaros stayed with 14-inch wheels and tires. The Camaro's engines were further awakened by the introduction of an air-conditioning cut-out switch, which shut off the air conditioning at full throttle.

Another banner year for sales, 192,219 Camaros rolled out of the Norwood and Van Nuys factories. A strong economy, an improving Camaro, and the revival of the American musclecar car market can be attributed for the surge in sales. After years of fast-looking but slow-going ponycars, buyers snapped up the new fuel-injected wonders. The Mustang GT and Dodge Daytona turbo had strong sales in 1986 as well, and it was no accident.

Calling All Cars

As more V-8-powered, rear-wheel-drive sedans were converted to front-wheel drive and V-6 power in the 1980s, police departments across the country were faced with a dilemma. How do you conduct a high-speed pursuit if your police car can't achieve high speed?

As the old cliché goes, if you can't beat 'em, join 'em. Although Chevrolet had flirted briefly with the idea of a police Camaro in 1979, Ford had blazed the trail in 1982 and 1983 with a stripped-down Mustang LX 5.0-liter equipped for law enforcement duty. The Mustangs were the clunky-looking sedans, not the hatch-backs, and were fitted with such heavy-duty items as oil coolers and silicone radiator hoses. Obviously no paddy wagon, the Mustang was used almost exclusively for highway patrol use, where high-speed ability was more important than passenger space. A black-and-white Mustang with lights on top proved to be a nice deterrent to speeders, and police Mustangs became a common sight.

With an increasingly fast Camaro in the fleet and a death struggle with Ford for law enforcement fleet sales supremacy, Chevrolet trotted out its own high-speed pursuit vehicle: the Camaro. The Camaro was in many ways even better suited than the Mustang for this specialized duty. The Camaro's better aerodynamics and more sophisticated suspension allowed a top speed of over 140 miles per hour, and the car presented a much more intimidating profile. The RPO B4C police package was introduced on the 1991 Camaro RS.

The police package carried all the heavy-duty gear that could be packed in a Camaro. For 1992, the Camaro Special Service Package included a choice of the 5.0-liter TPI with five-speed or the 5.7-liter TPI V-8 with automatic and a performance suspension, 16-inch wheels with P245/50ZR16 tires, four-wheel disc brakes, dual performance exhaust with dual catalytic converters, a limited-slip rear axle, engine oil cooler, 150-amp alternator, heavy-duty battery, and air conditioning.

As the cheap and moderately practical Fox-chassis Mustang went out of production in 1993, the Camaro took its place as the pursuit vehicle of choice. Ford declined to produce a pursuit Mustang after redesigning the car for 1994, concentrating instead on Crown Victorias and Explorer special service packages. The Camaro has since taken over that side of the business as the new intimidator.

The Chevrolet Special Service Camaro was introduced in 1991 for police use nationwide. An unconventional cop car, the Camaro was primarily used by highway patrol departments for high-speed pursuit—or as an intimidator to discourage high-speed pursuit. The tall spoiler on the Z28 in the background was new for 1991. Detroit Public Library National Automotive History Collection

The Honorable Competition

Once again, as in the beginning of the Camaro's life, Ford's Mustang was a competitor to be reckoned with. While the Mustang had for the most part shriveled into a sad Pinto clone in the 1970s, by the time the mid-1980s rolled around, the Mustang GT had firmly secured a fresh reputation for offering the most musclecar bang for the buck. In 1986, the 5.0-liter Mustang also offered electronic fuel injection with a 200-horsepower punch, along with less weight and a lower price than comparable Camaros. For 1987, the Mustang jumped to 225 horsepower thanks to a revised intake manifold and a freer-flowing head design. Ford also ran the Mustang back through the stylists barn for 1987, and the car emerged with a rounded nose, prominent ground effects, larger rear spoiler, and unique taillamp treatment. They also upgraded the interior while they were at it, so the Mustang's dash no longer looked like the Fairmont clone it had always been. And Dodge was even starting to reassert itself. The front-wheel-drive Daytona offered good power and economy thanks to the wonders of turbocharging. Sure, the Camaro Z28 was more sophisticated, handled better than the Mustang, and was no slouch in acceleration, but for the most part, the type of buyer shopping for Mustang GTs or Camaro Z28s has quarter-mile ETs and dollar signs on his mind.

Chevrolet people were well aware of the challenge presented by the 5.0-liter Mustang. "One of the things that 5.0-liter had—the free spin-up time on that engine is ridiculously quick," Camaro chief engineer Chuck Hughes recalled. "That is *really* a quick engine. You tap the throttle, and that engine is *right there,* like it didn't have a flywheel. And that's something the Camaro never had. We looked at free-throttle run-up and evaluated all the things that caused it to be slow responding, and it got into fuel management, timing, and advance; it was a complex group of reasons why that happened. But Ford had it. That 5.0-liter GT engine was a quick-responding engine. And in a light car like that, it made the acceleration really impressive. Now, if you look at the raw numbers, of 0–60 and times in the quarter, Camaro is more than competitive. But it didn't feel like it—it felt real smooth and not snappy. Boy, that GT was snappy, let me tell you. We could never get that in the Camaro," he said. "The first 100 feet in that car was really impressive. And it was for a bargain price. So that GT was really a winner." Those concerns would definitely figure into the blueprint for the next-generation Camaro, with happy results. But before that, the competitive pressures of the 5.0 Mustang led to the welcome return of the 350-cubic inch small-block in the Camaro.

The 350, or 5.7-liter, as it was officially christened, first arrived under third-generation Camaro hoods in the 1987 IROC Z28. The 5.7-liter used in the Camaro was basically the L89 Corvette engine with choked-down exhaust to fit in the F-body and cast-iron heads instead of aluminum. It produced 225 horsepower but was only available with automatic transmission. Still, the 350 finally allowed the new Camaro to crack the 15-second barrier in the quarter mile. *Musclecar Review* magazine, in its May, 1987 issue, clocked a 14.88 quarter mile at 92.87 miles per hour—still not enough to catch the 5.0-liter GT and LX 5.0 tested in the same issue, though, largely because the injected 302 Ford V-8 had bulked up to 225 horsepower that year.

Other magazines were noticing how the Camaro and Firebird were offering distinct driving experiences, especially with the proliferation of performance models. Chevrolet had the Z28 and the IROC Z28, while Pontiac had the Trans-Am, GTA, and the Firebird Formula. "But you do notice a difference in performance characteristics from make to make," noted *Automobile* magazine staffers in their May 1987 issue. "Slide over from the Firebird Formula to the IROC-Z; the Camaro's 5.0-liter V-8 feels a touch livelier, a shade sharper. And the 5.7-liter IROC-Z duly feels like a gutsier beast than the GTA. You know you're in the big mother of the bunch in the large-engined IROC."

Another old Camaro friend that returned for 1987 was a cloth top. A 350-cubic inch V-8 Camaro with a convertible top had last been available in 1969, so people could be forgiven for wondering if 1987 wasn't some new golden age of musclecars. Of course, things had changed considerably since 1969. Making a Camaro convertible was no easy thing, since the third-generation Camaro had not been designed with a convertible model in mind. In fact, this newest convertible wasn't even made by Chevrolet. They were constructed by Automobile Specialty Company (ASC), a long-time provider of sunroofs and specialty convertible conversions. For the Camaro, orders were channeled through Chevrolet, which sent the cars to ASC. ASC cut the top and installed various chassis-reinforcement

The Camaro GTZ aerodynamic 4.3-liter V-6 concept car illustrated how the Camaro might someday punch a cleaner hole through the atmosphere. The 4.3-liter V-6 was never installed in the Camaro, but Chevrolet had reasons to showcase the engine. Besides showing how future Z28s might still be formidable performance cars even if OPEC once again closed the oil spigot, the 4.3 V-6 was also Chevrolet's engine in NASCAR Busch Grand National competition. A little more exposure never hurt. *Roger Huntington Collection/Dobbs Publishing Group*

hardware, then shipped the car to the ordering dealer approximately $4,400 heavier.

While the engineering group wrestled with the problem of regaining street supremacy, there were competitors on the race track to contend with, as well. "When I was chief engineer at Camaro and Firebird, we tried to support the people who raced the cars," Hughes said. "I used to tell the group, 'I don't give a damn if you win the race, from me personally, I just don't want you to break. I want you to finish the race. You guys worry about winning the race—you tell me what breaks, and I'll fix the damn things.' And I hired Bill Mitchell out of Connecticut to go tell me, in engineering terms," he said.

"So he would buy the cars, get the drivers, campaign the cars, document what broke, and get the data back to me. I'd redesign the parts and get them validated (with his help many times) and get them released," Hughes said. Some of the problems for SCCA, IMSA, and Canadian Player's Challenge Camaro racers were failed coils, busted pulleys, and failed fifth gears. "We did about 18 or 20 changes on the production car, and the guys would say, 'We just had to put a roll bar in them and race 'em,'" Hughes said.

"We had to do it in our spare time. Nobody gave us any time for that kind of stuff. But, God, you've got accelerated testing there. Why not use the information?" Hughes continued. "I'd go to races and talk to somebody and say, 'Who do you think is going to win the race?' And they'd say, 'Well, the Camaros are out there in front now, but the Porsches will be there at the end.' And I told our guys, 'We can't have that. The Camaros have got to be there at the end. They're the tractors.'"

Chevrolet went further helping racers than just analyzing what parts broke. In 1988, Chevy quietly released the first handful of "1LE" race-ready Camaros, noteworthy for having nonessential accessories deleted to save weight and improve serviceability, along with providing such necessities as an oil cooler, four-wheel disc brakes, and a performance axle.

General Motors, indeed most large corporations, are often seen as faceless, mind-warping work camps, but real people with real enthusiasm work there, and sometimes that genuine human touch shines through. Such was the case with the development of the 1LE Camaros.

Chevrolet Powertrain Manager Ray Canale and Chuck Hughes put together the 1LE package largely in their spare time with help from a promising young student, Mark Stielow, from the University of Missouri-Rolla. Hughes was on GM executive Lloyd Reuss' team on college relations in the 1980s, with one of his duties being to help with the scholarship program. He would interview perhaps 12 or 13 people for four or five full-blown GM scholarships, and for the other students he would try to have "outstanding" summer jobs available if they wanted them.

Stielow was one such scholarship candidate, but one with a definite knack for high-performance. As Hughes remembers it, "I said, 'Mark, in case you're not selected, here are a couple of jobs in the corporation that you might be considered for summer employment, and would you be interested?' And one of them was to help Ray Canale, our powertrain manager, and myself, with defining the problems that the guys were having during racing and also get a 1LE package released. Well, his reply back was, 'I don't really need this scholarship. Why don't you just take me off the list of candidates. I want your summer job!'" Hughes said.

"As a sophomore in college, you couldn't tell him from a seasoned engineer," Hughes recalled. "He was all over the place. And he helped us get that through the system and get the parts allocated and designed and available—and took the parts to the plant in Van Nuys and did the production tryout, as basically a sophomore in college. He and Ray Canale were the ones who pulled that through."

The 1LE package was especially helpful to racers in the SCCA Escort Endurance and IMSA Firehawk series, plus the Player's Challenge in Canada. Weight reduction came by deleting air conditioning and heater components, deleting fog lamps, and switching to an aluminum driveshaft. Both the 305 and 350 V-8s were available in 1LE trim. With the "G92" performance axle, a few suspension tweaks, and big four-wheel disc brakes, the 1LE cars required a lot less track prep than Camaros of the recent past.

Some 1LE parts even had multiple uses. "The aluminum prop shaft was a weight reduction item that was used on the production car too," Hughes said. "We sold a lot of cars with aluminum prop shafts, aluminum brake drums on the back. The reason was that we had to keep it in a weight category for EPA fuel economy, and when you ordered vehicles with T-tops, it would push it out of the category. In order for a guy to get a full car with T-tops and stay in that weight category, we'd have to put in weight-reduction items like aluminum prop shafts."

General Motors later devised other ways to help the third-generation Camaros in the horsepower wars. The GM Motorsports Technology Group offered a high-output, 5.7-liter V-8 crate engine for retrofit in 1982 to 1987 Camaros originally equipped with the 305 V-8 and automatic. The 5.7 was emissions legal when installed in the cars as specified and helped the Camaro regain some of its reputation on the street.

Slowly, the scrutiny given to the Camaro's high-performance abilities paid off, and Camaros started becoming a force on the road courses of the United States and

Canada. In 1986, Wally Dallenbach Jr. won the SCCA Trans-Am Championship in a Camaro, and Jack Baldwin was a five-time winner behind the wheel of a Camaro in IMSA GTO. He was a three-time GTO winner in 1987, while Willy T. Ribbs also took Camaros to victory in IMSA GTO. In the IMSA Firestone Firehawk series, Scott Flanders and Skip Gunnell won the Sports class at Sebring in a Z28, and John Heinricy and Mitch Wright won the Grand Sports class in an IROC-Z.

Heinricy and Don Knowles slaughtered the field in the 1989 SCCA Escort Endurance GT Class championship in their Camaro. In 1990, the IMSA Grand Sports class winners at Sebring were Joe Varde and Don Wallace in an IROC-Z. In the increasingly wild GTO category, Gregg Pickett and Tommy Riggins scored a class win and fifth overall at the annual 12-hour Sebring event. In 1991, Lou Gigliotti won the SCCA World Challenge Super Sport Class in his Young Chevrolet Camaro. The Camaro had long been the best handling American sport coupe, and with the bugs finally worked out it started to show it at the race track.

Regulatory Shuffle

As the Camaro's street performance steadily improved throughout the decade, fans of the car could be forgiven for scratching their heads at the proliferation of different engine and transmission combinations and the variety of horsepower ratings the various V-8s produced. Buyers must have surely often wondered why this engine was only available with an automatic transmission, while *that* engine could be ordered with a manual transmission. As is often the case when something makes no sense, the federal government played a role.

Hughes explained GM's dilemma as: "What we can sell that the customer wants and avoid the gas-guzzler law. We did not want to exceed that," he said. "If you did, you had to pay fines. It was a corporate policy that we would not be selling anything that you had to pay fines on. It was just a bad image.

"So we had a lot of engines released for the car—way more than we wanted to—that is, different versions of engines so that we fit ourselves around a pattern that would avoid gas-guzzler and still provide what the customer wanted. It was a really tough assignment," Hughes said.

In 1988, the most recognized model in Camaro history, the Z28, was for the second time retired. Taking its place as the performance-oriented Camaro was the IROC-Z. Considering Chevrolet's substantial investment in the IROC racing series, the change probably made sense at the time, although sweeping aside an icon like the Z28 Camaro, even if the cars were essentially the same, was not Chevrolet's best move of the 1980s. Indeed, the Z28 was back after two short years.

And ultimately, the IROC may not have helped the Camaro's image. While racing fans knew IROC stood for the International Race of Champions, a racing series that pitted the best drivers in the world against each other in identically-prepared Camaros, to many casual observers "IROC-Z" sounded like some sort of cheesy rock 'n roll model—the 1980s equivalent to the often stereotyped, wildly-striped Pontiac Trans-Ams of the disco era.

In any event, with a new Camaro still a few years down the road, each new model year brought further tweaks and refinements. The Z28 may have been gone, but buyers could outfit a base Sport Coupe with a 170-horsepower, 305-inch V-8 and manual transmission, surpassing what was available in the Z28 only a few years earlier. In 1989, a PASS-key theft-deterrent system became standard equipment. The next generation of sound equipment, the compact disc player, was turning vinyl records into instant antiques in the late 1980s, and a CD player joined the Camaro option list in 1989. Also that year a resurrected RS model became the base Camaro. The base RS coupe started at $11,495, while the RS convertible listed for $16,995.

In 1990, the entry-level Camaro engine, the 2.8-liter V-6, was hogged out to 3.1 liters, giving the base RS 140 horsepower. The LB9 and L98 V-8s switched to a speed-density fuel-injection system as available engine-management computing power increased. To comply with the new federal laws, Chevrolet added a driver's-side airbag to the Camaro as standard equipment. And then, just like that, the Z28 was back.

The Z28 returned thanks to a severing of the relationship between Chevrolet and IROC. Evidently the financial cost required to remain the series sponsor was more than Chevrolet wanted to shoulder. That left a bit of a problem though. Chevrolet's license to use the IROC label expired at the end of 1989, and the 1990 models were already in production. Once the clock struck 1990, Chevrolet could no longer sell an IROC-Z Camaro.

What to do? In Chevrolet's case, revive the Z28 and dramatically accelerate the

1991 Camaro's introduction. The 1990 model year for the Camaro officially ended at the end of 1989. In March 1990, production started on the 1991 Camaros, which had a few new features to distinguish them. The 1991 Z28 coupe sported a tall wing on the rear deck instead of the old spoiler and had new ground-effects panels and revised scoopettes on the hood. The Firebird, although not facing the same IROC problems as the Camaro, was also worked over, and received a new nose piece and side skirts. Camaro performance remained steady, with the top engine option continuing to be the 245-horsepower 5.7-liter small-block.

As the lame duck before the new Camaro was to be introduced, the 1992 models don't differ much from the 1991s. But 1992 was the 25th anniversary year for the Camaro, so Chevrolet commemorated the milestone by introducing a Heritage appearance package. The $175 Heritage package was available on all models, but only with Arctic White, Bright Red, and Black color schemes. The package included special twin striping on the hood, deck lid, and spoiler, a body-color grille, and blacked-out headlamp pockets. All Camaros got a 25th anniversary instrument panel badge.

As the 1982–1992 Camaro reign came to an end, there was some final glory. Scott Sharp won the SCCA Trans-Am championship in 1991 in a Camaro, and teammate Jack Baldwin won the 1992 championship in his Hot Wheels Camaro. He won only two races, at Watkins Glen and Trois-Rivieres, but four second-place finishes and two other top-fives kept him in the hunt. He never finished lower than seventh all year.

The Archer brothers, Tommy and Bobby, joined the Trans-Am circuit in 1992 driving Dodge Daytonas. For the first time in a long time, the Trans-Am series resembled the factory-backed battlefields of the Trans-Am's glory days of the late 1960s and early 1970s. In both 1992 and 1993, all top-10 points finishers piloted either Camaros, Mustangs, or Daytonas.

And so, after two fuel crises, a couple recessions, and six presidents, all was much as it had been 25 years earlier: high-powered Camaros and Mustangs dueling on the street and on the track. And the scary part was, things were about to get even more competitive. . . .

With a weak domestic economy on one side and a high price tag of $21,500 on the other, Chevrolet squeezed out only 1,254 convertibles Z28s for 1992—but what a ride! By the end of the third generation Camaro's run, the car boasted a fuel-injected 350-cubic inch V-8, 16-inch wheels, and assorted special high-performance options. The car had come a long way since the 1982 Z28's base engine, rated at only 145 horsepower. *Chevrolet*

6

Chapter
Six

The General Strikes Back:
1993 on

With 11 model years to its credit, the third-generation Camaros lasted nearly as long as the 1970s-generation cars. Both generations were extraordinarily long-lived, especially for sporty cars, where styles change nearly as fast as clothing fashions. Along the way, the third-generation Camaros ran the gamut from stone to stormer. Starting life in late 1981 as anemic pretenders endowed with razor sharp handling, they ended their run as 14-second drag strip performers endowed with even sharper handling characteristics, available in coupe or convertible form.

Still, after 11 years, there were several areas ready for an upgrade. As always, safety and emission standards were getting increasingly strict. There remained new handling frontiers to conquer, and if the Camaro was going to turn heads like it used to, it needed a new suit of sheet metal. The 1982 Camaro was a knockout when it was introduced, but even a super model loses her impact if she wears the same clothes to work every day for 11 years. Third-generation Camaro sales had declined steadily since their mid-1980s peak, and if the car was to survive, it needed a boost in the marketplace.

But it was Ford's Mustang that once again laid down the real challenge by offering more horsepower for less money. Drag strips teemed with stripped-down, hopped-up 5.0-liter Mustangs, and while clearly not every Camaro buyer cared about quarter-mile times and automotive rivalries, gearheads are often opinion makers, particularly when it comes to sporting transportation. The word on the street was the Mustang was cheaper and faster; sure the Camaro handled better and was more sophisticated, and some top-line Z28s were quicker, but that

didn't make Johnny Camaro feel any better when he watched Joe Mustang's taillights receding in the distance.

In other words, all that was needed was a Camaro that was faster, cheaper, safer, cleaner and better looking. Is that all?

To Chevrolet's credit, they hit most of these goals. The new Z28's base price of $16,779 offered a lot of go for the dough. Difficult as it might be to top the boy-racer visual appeal of the 1982–1992 models, the fourth-generation Camaros made the previous cars look almost tame. With its tapered nose, sweeping 68-degree windshield angle and massive wheels, the 1993 Camaro came across from certain angles like some rolling Hot Wheels toy, the sort of car that fired the imagination of the inner notebook-doodling child in us all.

The Z28 model was almost low key in its styling, for a change, with few external differences between it and the base car. The Z28 used a blacked-out C-pillar and had its own aluminum wheels plus assorted Z28 emblems. Standard rolling stock with the Z28 were P235/55R16 tires; P245/50ZR16s were optional. The base car had a body-colored C-pillar and smaller wheels.

The 1993 Camaro was as visually hot-blooded as Detroit iron gets, although some of the form didn't necessarily improve the function. With a drag coefficient of .34 the new Camaro looked a bit more aerodynamic than it really was, and while the car appeared smaller, it was actually larger than the previous car. The 1993 Camaro continued with a 101-inch wheelbase, but overall length gained nearly an inch, to 193 inches long, and width expanded by nearly 2 inches. Curb weight came in at slightly over 3,400 pounds for the Z28. Also, there was no

Chevrolet released this teaser photo in 1992 to whet the public's appetite for the forthcoming new Camaro. Ford was trying to prop up the aging Mustang line with a new Cobra model, while working on its new-for-1994 design, and this brief glimpse must have given them a cold, clammy feeling. All fourth-generation Camaro and Firebird production was shifted to St. Therese, Quebec, Canada. A slow product rollout contributed to low production figures for 1993. *Chevrolet*

were also different, having rear outlets as opposed to the center outlets of the Corvette's manifolds. And the Corvette was lubed with synthetic oil.

Additionally, the engine accessories were mounted on the right in the Camaro, but on the left for the 'Vette. The Corvette used a remote-mounted electric air injection reaction (AIR) pump, while the Camaro's pump was mounted to the engine block. Visually, the Camaro was adorned with less-expensive, stamped-steel valve covers, while the Corvette got the pricier composite covers. Finally, the Corvette's injectors were covered with a "beauty shield"; the Camaro's injectors were exposed.

The base model Camaro was stronger for 1993, as well. The 3.1-liter V-6 used in 1992 was punched out to 3.4 liters, nudging horsepower up to 160. Both base model and Z28 benefited from a much stiffer body structure—23 percent stiffer by Chevrolet's reckoning. The Camaro's suspension also ditched the MacPherson strut front suspension of the third-generation cars, for a short-long-arm front suspension (SLA). To keep costs in line, the Camaro still did not have an independent rear suspension, but the multi-link system with trailing arms worked so well, few could tell the difference.

But the Camaro wasn't all muscle. To appease the federal regulators and polish the good-corporate-citizen image, the 1993 Camaro was equipped with dual front air bags, and CFC-free air conditioning. Anti-lock brakes were standard equipment, as Chevrolet was pushing at the time for all its cars to be so equipped. The dual air bags and CFC-free air weren't available on the Mustang until the following year. Anti-lock brakes were optional on the Mustang.

In keeping with recent tradition, the 1993 Camaro paced the Indianapolis 500 that May. Chevrolet General Manager Jim Perkins drove the car on the pace laps. Once again, a Pace Car replica was offered, a $995 option available on the Z28. Whereas earlier Pace Cars were brightly-hued affairs, the 1993 Pace Car adopted the night fighter look. All were black over white, with white wheels and thin yellow, red, and green stripes and graphics. Inside there was matching seat upholstery. In all, 633 were built, making the 1993 editions the second most-exclusive of the four Camaro Pace Cars.

With an all-new Camaro on the street, comparisons with the Mustang and Firebird were inevitable, and the early magazine tests of the 1993 Z28 quickly confirmed

Camaro convertible available for 1993, although T-tops were an option. The ragtop arrived the following year.

But looks weren't the only feature of the new Z28 to entice enthusiasts to reach for their checkbooks. Under the hood was a version of the Corvette's own LT1 5.7-liter V-8, an engine that represented the pinnacle of small-block development. The LT1 was good for 275 horsepower in the Camaro, 40 more horsepower than was available in the top-of-the-line Mustang Cobra. Adding to the appeal of the powertrain was a new Borg-Warner T56 six-speed manual transmission, although production problems initially kept those in short supply.

The new Camaro shared its V-8 soul with the Corvette, but there were differences between the 'Vette's LT1 and the version in the Camaro. Most were for packaging reasons; others were cost-saving measures. The Z28's LT1 block had two-bolt main-bearing caps, while the Corvette's had four-bolt mains. The Camaro had a single three-way catalyst with single pipes entering and exiting, while the Corvette rumbled on with dual catalysts. The Camaro's exhaust manifolds

seat-of-the-pants impressions. *Car and Driver* recorded a 14.0 quarter mile at 100 miles per hour, compared to the 1993 Mustang Cobra's 14.3 at 98 miles per hour. Handling prowess was pegged at .92 g on the skid pad. Top speed was clocked at 154 miles per hour. The *C&D* staff backed up their quarter-mile time with a 14.1 ET 10 months later when the redesigned 215-horsepower 1994 Mustang GT was introduced, smoking the Mustang's 14.9-second quarter mile. Almost overnight, Chevrolet had shifted the balance of power in the modern musclecar wars.

More Good News

If there was one thing missing from the 1993 Camaro's rebirth, it was a cloth top. Since its reintroduction in 1987, the convertible top had reinvigorated the Camaro line-up. A droptop fourth-generation car had been planned all along, although the doing took a little longer than the planning. The new convertible finally arrived for the 1994 model, available in base or Z28 models. Unlike the previous Camaro convertibles, which were farmed out to ASC for conversion, the 1994 models were built in-house at the St. Therese assembly plant, although ASC supplied the top and bracing.

This latest convertible was more civilized than previous editions. Included as standard equipment were a three-piece hard tonneau cover, a full headliner, and a heated glass backlight. The Camaro convertible weighed some 150 pounds heavier than a comparable coupe, thanks to extra structural bracing and beefier cross-members. That all helped stop the traditional convertible shakes, but it also weighed down performance. *Car and Driver* recorded a 14.6-second quarter mile at 97 miles per hour, about a half-second off the coupe's pace.

The further refinement for 1994 was the introduction of an electronically controlled four-speed automatic transmission. Replacing the 4L60 unit, the new 4L60-E was another example of the revolution in

Camaro versus Mustang—the Final Trans-Am Battles

Although factory participation in the SCCA's Trans-Am series has ebbed and flowed over the course of 30-plus years, some of the best toe-to-toe Chevy versus Ford battles of all time took place during the fourth-generation Camaro's time in the sun. The new Camaro was a winner immediately, with Buz McCall's stable of Camaros successfully fending off well-funded and ably-driven Mustangs fielded by Tom Gloy and Jack Roush teams.

Of course, by the 1990s, there was little in common between street Camaros and Trans-Am Camaros, unlike in earlier days when both the series and the car were young. Trans-Am Camaros and Mustangs evolved through the years into little more than tube-frame NASCAR stockers covered by stock-appearing sheet metal. Were there any real differences between the two? Trans-Am champion (1989) Dorsey Schroeder raced both Mustangs and Camaros in the 1990s, including Jim Derhaag's Camaro in 1993 and Tom Gloy Mustangs in 1994, and seemed like a reasonable person to ask. At the 1994 Dallas Grand Prix we put the question to him.

"The Mustang's big advantage has been we've always had top end on the Chevy. We've always got a mile or two an hour more than they do, but they seem, on long tracks, to have a better ET on the straightaways. Like in drag racing, we get the big number at the end, but they pull the ET," he said.

"Having driven Derhaag's Camaro last year and being back in the Ford this year, the primary difference isn't the body as much as it's the motors. The Chevy's got a broader powerband than the Ford. The Ford's got top-end grunt," he said. "Overall it's really pretty close."

Minor differences or no, the fourth-generation Camaros made an immediate impact in Trans-Am in 1993. Scott Sharp won his second Trans-Am title in the Rain-X Camaro that year, with wins at Mosport, Sears Point, Toronto, Watkins Glen, Trois Rivieres, and Road America. Scott Pruett then claimed his second SCCA Trans-Am championship in a Buz McCall Camaro in 1994.

Chevrolet dropped its factory backing in the SCCA Trans-Am series after the 1996 season, deciding there were better ways to spend sponsorship dollars and thus handed the 1997 title to Tom Kendall and Ford. Perhaps Chevrolet will one day again back Camaro drivers in this series. If not, it would be a great shame. After all, for three decades the Trans-Am has been the prime arena for Mustangs and Camaros to beat up on each other, a battle Chevrolet usually won. That's a lot of bragging rights to just walk away from.

1992 SCCA Trans-Am champion Jack Baldwin slides around a corner at the 1994 Grand Prix of Dallas. That year Scott Pruett won the SCCA Trans-Am drivers' championship behind the wheel of a Camaro.

The 1994 Camaro convertible chassis was stiffened with reinforced rocker panels, a connecting brace between the rear wheelwells, heavier-duty front cross-members, and engine-cradle reinforcement. The new convertibles all had power tops, headliners, and heated rear windows. *Chevrolet*

powertrain refinement brought about by the computer. The 4L60-E's Powertrain Control Module (PCM) was capable of measuring throttle position, engine load, vehicle speed, and gear range to give optimum shifting ability. The transmission even featured an altitude compensator and over-rev protection for extreme conditions.

With the high-end cars squared away, the base coupes were given a boost in 1995. Midway through the year, Buick's 3.8-liter, 200-horsepower V-6 became available in the Camaro. The 3.8 was only a $350 option and was well worth the extra money, offering 40 more horsepower than the Chevy 3.4-liter V-6. The 3.8 became the standard Camaro engine for 1996, giving the base car more horsepower than many of the top-line Z28s of the 1970s. Another development for 1995 was the introduction of traction control, or "Accelerated Slip Regulation," a useful option for owners of Z28s who lived in snowy, wet climes.

An old nickname from the past was resurrected again, in 1996, with the return of the RS to the line-up. A separate model, the RS had its own ground effects and spoiler, along with RS front and rear fascias.

It would have been easy to rest on these laurels and coast the rest of the way through the fourth-generation Camaro's life cycle, having dispatched with the Mustang (if not in sales, in speed) and raised the bar for affordable performance cars. But among

performance buyers (and enthusiastic engineers) too much power is never enough. This time, however, much like in the old days of Yenko and Nickey, the next level of Camaro performance came from an outside source—SLP Engineering. SLP was founded in 1986 by Ed Hamburger as Street Legal Performance, with the goal of developing aftermarket parts that met OE standards of performance. The company's first factory program was the 1992 Pontiac Firebird Firehawk and later the WS-6, with SLP helping return the Firebird to its Ram-Air heritage.

A relationship with Chevrolet grew out of SLP's dealings with Pontiac. "We had a strong sales success," said Reg Harris, director of marketing at SLP. "We went from 25 units the first year, to 200, to 500, to 750. And then we went from 750 to 5,100, to last year [1997, when] we did 8,000 cars," he said.

For Chevrolet, a parallel program seemed ideal. It would keep the Firebird from being the undisputed master of the F-car ranks and would allow Chevrolet to further tie the new Camaro to its musclecar past by resurrecting the SS label. And so the SS was reborn, although creating a new factory/outsider hybrid was no simple engine swap as in days of yore. "We had to meet GM standards, meet the GM validation schedule for crash worthiness and reliability," Harris said.

The SS package SLP developed relied heavily on traditional hot-rodding techniques and closely paralleled the Firehawk modifications. First up was the big power number, 305 horsepower, thanks to a functional hood scoop and forced-air-induction system. Other standard SS pieces included a restyled deck lid spoiler, a lightly-modified suspension with SLP-designed links, 17x9-inch, ZR-1-styled, cast-aluminum alloy wheels with BFGoodrich P245/40ZR17 Comp T/A tires, exterior and interior SS badges, and a Camaro SS console plaque. Base price for the package was $3,999.

For even better performance and looks, SLP offered nine options for the SS: a Hurst shifter, a free-flowing exhaust that bumped horsepower up to 310, a Torsen differential for $699, or Auburn differential, chrome wheels, two up-level suspension packages with Bilstein dampers, a key fob, a dash plaque, a car cover, floor mats, and a synthetic oil lube package.

Although SLP handled the modifications, the Camaro SS was ordered through the regular Chevrolet dealer network. (This new SS was never referred to as a "Super Sport," as earlier models were.) The first Camaro SSs were shipped in October 1995 as 1996 models. By the time the 1996 run was complete, SLP had shipped 2,410 Camaro SSs out the door. Although the SS option may have been a bit pricey for the average enthusiast, the acceptance of the SS was not surprising. The performance increase was real. *Car and Driver* conducted two tests of the 1996 Camaro SS and clocked quarter-mile ETs of 13.6 seconds at 106 miles per hour and 13.7 at 102. Like the long-retired SS logo, performance numbers like that had not been seen since big-block V-8s hid under Camaro hoods.

Future Collectibles

Although there are fewer performance cars to choose from in the modern era—at least compared with the musclecar golden age of the 1960s—there is still some 1990s machinery that will likely entice future collectors. Many of those will be late 1990s Camaros.

After a one-year absence, the Z28 convertible returned to the Camaro line-up in 1994. With a full headliner, the 1994 convertible was a lot more civilized than earlier topless Camaros. It was also pricier. At $22,075 the ragtop commanded a $5,000 premium over the base Z28 coupe. *Chevrolet*

The Corvette super-tuners at Callaway Cars tore themselves away from Chevy's fiberglass sports car long enough, starting in 1995, to put together a SuperNatural Camaro package, consisting of an eight-piece composite body kit and hardware that could be configured a number of different ways. Callaway offered two suspension packages, Brembo brakes, and, best of all, a 404-horsepower, 383-cubic inch Chevy V-8.

In 1997, Chevrolet celebrated the Camaro's 30th birthday with an anniversary option to commemorate the event. Like aerodynamic blasts from the past, the anniversary Camaros were draped in white paint with Hugger Orange stripes, as used on 1969 Indy Pace Cars. Overall, the visual effect of orange over white was perhaps better suited to the older cars, but the look was still striking. Chevrolet even revived the houndstooth upholstery pattern for the interior and dressed it up with 30th anniversary logos. White wheels added to the effect.

"I may be biased, but I'm betting that both of them, the [anniversary] SS and Z28, will one day take their places among the most desirable of all Camaros," predicted Chevrolet General Manager John Middlebrook in a 1997 Camaro SS dealer video.

Even among the new SS Camaros there are special editions. In 1997, SLP concocted a limited run of Camaro SSs powered by the LT4 V-8—no small thing, since the 330-horsepower LT4 engine was itself a limited-edition powerplant for the Corvette. "We did 100 for the U.S. Camaro market, 29 Firehawks for the U.S. market, and 6 SS models for Canada," Reg Harris said.

Making the LT4 conversion happen was a different matter than creating the standard SS package. "Quite a bit of cooperation was required from GM and SPO [Service Parts Operations]," Harris said. "You would order

The SS name reappeared on the Camaro in 1996, thanks to SLP Engineering. The distinctive hood scoop set the SS apart from the standard Z28 plus provided a fresh-air intake for a horsepower boost. SLP's sales and engineering operations are in Troy, Michigan, while most parts manufacturing takes place in New Jersey. The bulk of the work on the cars takes place in LaSalle, Canada, near Montreal. *Courtesy SLP Engineering*

an SS, and the SS has special coding on it, and we did engine swaps at our plant in Montreal. And then it was shipped by SLP to the dealer from Canada—not by GM, but by SLP," Harris said. "We balanced and blueprinted them, and we conservatively rated it at 330 horsepower." (The 330-horsepower Corvette LT4 had a more open exhaust, a different cam, and unique electrical control unit [ECU]. SLP's tinkering brought the LT4 in the Camaro back up to the 330-horsepower rating.)

Another special SLP Camaro was created for Chevrolet dealer and NASCAR Winston Cup team owner Rick Hendrick. Hendrick requested a limited run of his own 30th anniversary SS cars for special customers. Nine were built. "They were silver and black, and they also had special badging, special car covers, [and] special floor mats," Harris said. "There was a B-pillar plaque for Hendrick Motorsports on it. That same logo style was carried over on the key fob and car cover and floor mats."

"Hendrick flew the people in that bought the nine cars, and we signed the cars. Terry Labonte was there; Rick was there; Jim Perkins was there," Harris said. The cars were special in more ways than one, selling for a little over $47,000, which included lunch at Charlotte Motor Speedway with Labonte and a Speedway tour. Hendrick saved a little of the event for himself. "Rick's got car number one down at his museum in Harrisburg, North Carolina," Harris said.

After the improvements Chevrolet worked into the 1998 Camaro, the need for special editions may diminish. The 1998 Z28 was equipped with a new LS1 V-8 that produced 305 horsepower in standard trim. That's more than twice the standard horsepower offered in the 1982 Z28, to shine a little perspective on the state of modern high-performance.

The LS1 was a lot more than just a small-block Chevy with a hot cam and big valves. It was essentially an all-new engine. The LS1's features included an aluminum, deep-skirt engine block, a "specific contour diecast-aluminum oil pan" that added to the engine's structural rigidity, a composite intake manifold, larger muffler volume, a heavily revised electronics package (with an individual coil for each cylinder), and an equally revised fuel system.

The claimed advantages of the LS1 were quieter performance, improved durability, and improved warm-up and drive-

SLP's forced-air-induction system for the Camaro SS helped boost the LT1 V-8 to 305 horsepower and was the heart of the SS package. SLP's engine massaging was even more impressive considering the OBD-II (On-Board Diagnostics, Second-Generation) engine management came on-board in 1996, as stricter emissions regulations took effect. *SLP Engineering*

For 1998 the Camaro received a new face with a more traditional open-mouth grille, reminiscent of earlier Camaros. The grille masked a new LS1 V-8 as well, giving the Z28 305 standard horsepower. *Chevrolet*

ability. All that was true, but the real advantage was a stone-stock Z28 that could turn 13.8-second quarter miles all day and night, placing the 1998s among the very fastest Camaros ever built.

For those who needed a serious horsepower fix, the SS package returned, although with a slight difference in the way it was sold. "In the past when you ordered an SS, there was a base SS package that was tires, wheels, hood, deck-lid spoiler, exterior decals, induction system," Harris explained. "In 1998, that package continues to be produced and

Following pages
The rising popularity of the Brickyard 400 NASCAR Winston Cup race held at the Indianapolis Motor Speedway may someday help that race eclipse the venerable Indy 500. If so, the Brickyard 400 pace cars may also take their place alongside Indy 500 pace cars as musclecar collectibles of the first order. Camaros have served four times as the pace car for the Indianapolis 500, and for 1997 a Camaro set the pace for the NASCAR Indy event. Fifty-three festival cars for the 1997 NASCAR Brickyard 400 were built, all 30th anniversary models.

The 30th Anniversary 1997 Camaros were given the same white and orange striping scheme as the 1969 Indy Pace Cars. (Oddly, Chevrolet chose not to resurrect the blue and white colors used on the 1967 Pace Car.) The door handles were painted white, as were the five-spoke wheels and front fascia intake. Other 1997 changes included reconfigured front bucket seats, available Goodyear Eagle GS-C P245/50ZR-16 radials, and automatic daytime running lamps, a safety feature of dubious value, at best. *Chevrolet*

The 30th anniversary Camaro's upholstery featured a houndstooth pattern, as did the 1969 Indianapolis 500 Pace Car Camaro used for inspiration. A 30th anniversary logo on the seat headrests was also part of the $575 Anniversary package. *Chevrolet*

installed by SLP. The difference is, in 1997 that option package was shown on SLP's second window sticker. For 1998 that same window sticker item will be part of the Chevrolet portion of the window sticker. So in effect, in 1998 when the dealer orders an SS, his open account is debited by Chevrolet for the cost of the package. And Chevrolet pays SLP. In the past, SLP would bill the dealer direct."

The SS customer has also come into a little sharper focus. Most go for the SLP options and the GM options, like leather and the Bose stereo too. Whereas the original SS attracted a younger, less affluent buyer, the new SS customer is about a 40- to 55-year-old male who remembers the cars *when* and doesn't skimp now. "He's been successful in his business life, and this is his treat. He could have whatever car he wants. He could have a 'Vette; he could have a Cobra, but an SS is what he truly wants," Harris said.

Although most Camaros sold through the years have not been performance models, it is still the image and reputation of the various Super Sports, Z28s, Pace Cars, and IROC-Zs that have defined the Camaro and kept the car in the public eye. While other car fashions have changed, Camaro buyers still want powerful V-8s driving the rear wheels, preferably with a manual transmission between the two. Given the opportunity, they will buy performance.

"If you look at the impact of the SS," Harris said, "We ran about 13 percent of all Z28 volume last year [1997]. And overall, if you measure all the V-8 Firebirds, Trans-Ams, Formulas, Z28s, all of that, SLP modifications appeared on about 20 percent of all the V-8 F-cars."

Which is as it should be. As one of the last surviving musclecars with roots in the 1960s, it is only fitting that buyers still expect maximum performance from their Camaros. It is that expectation that has kept the Camaro alive for more than 30 years, while scores of lesser cars have faded away, lost in memory.

Camaro LT1 V-8 Spec sheet

Engine type	OHV V-8
Block	Cast-iron
Cylinder heads	Aluminum, 2 valves per cylinder
Bore x stroke (in)	4.00x3.48
Displacement	350 ci/5,737 cc
Compression ratio	10.5:1
Induction	SFI
Lifters	Hydraulic roller
Cam drive	Chain
Horsepower	275 @ 5,000 rpm
Torque	325 @ 2,000 rpm
Redline	5,700 rpm

With EPA mileage ratings of 18 miles per gallon city and 26 highway, the 1998 Z28 SS is stingier with fuel than any 1960s Camaro SS yet still capable of 13-second quarter miles. After the dark early-emission-control days of low-compression ratios and endless vacuum hoses, the revolution in computer processing has allowed engineers to tune cars for clean breath and vintage acceleration. *Courtesy SLP Engineering*

Appendices

Z28 Production Totals by Model Year, 1967–1974 and 1977–1996

1967	602
1968	7,199
1969	20,302
1970 1/2	8,733
1971	4,862
1972	2,575
1973	11,574
1974	13,802
1977	14,349
1978	54,907
1979	84,877
1980	45,137
1981	43,272
1982	71,242
1983	62,650
1984	100,899
1985	68,403
1986	88,132
1987	53,607*
1988	27,811*†
1989	24,007*†
1990	5,507*†
1991	15,655*
1992	6,451*
1993	17,850
1994	40,940*
1995	38,359*
1996	17,844*

* Includes convertible models
† IROC-Z

Camaro SS Production Totals by Model Year, 1967–1972, 1996–1997

1967	34,411
1968	30,695
1969	34,932
1970 1/2	12,476
1971	8,377
1972	6,562
1996	2,410*
1997	3,430*

* Z28 SS model, by SLP Engineering

Camaro Indy Pace Car Replica Production

1967	100 (approx.)*
1969 Z11 convert.	3,675
1969 Z10 coupe	Unknown
1982	6,360
1993	633

*Festival cars, not replicas

Camaro 1LE Production Totals

1988	4
1989	0
1990	62
1991	478
1992	705
1993	19
1994	135
1995	106

The Z28 could be fitted with dual four-barrel carburetors on a cross-ram intake for 1969.

SCCA Trans-Am champions (Camaro drivers)

Year	Driver	Victories
1968	Mark Donohue	10
1969	Mark Donohue	6
1983	David Hobbs	4
1986	Wally Dallenbach Jr.	4
1991	Scott Sharp	6
1992	Jack Baldwin	2
1993	Scott Sharp	6
1994	Scott Pruett	3

International Race of Champions (IROC) Series Champions: The Camaro Years (1974–1980, 1984–1989)

IROC II	(1975)	Bobby Unser
IROC III	(1976)	A. J. Foyt
IROC IV	(1977)	A. J. Foyt
IROC V	(1978)	Al Unser
IROC VI	(1979)	Mario Andretti
IROC VII	(1980)	Bobby Allison
IROC VIII	(1984)	Cale Yarborough
IROC IX	(1985)	Harry Gant
IROC X	(1986)	Al Unser Jr.
IROC XI	(1987)	Geoff Bodine
IROC XII	(1988)	Al Unser Jr.
IROC XIII	(1989)	Terry Labonte

Camaro High-Performance Engines, 1967–1998

Listed are high-performance V-8s with four-barrel carburetion or fuel injection, as available in Z28s, Super Sports, Rally Sports, IROC-Zs, and other performance models. Four-cylinder engines, six-cylinders, and two-barrel equipped V-8s not included.

Year	Displacement	Horsepower	Torque
1967			
Z28	302 ci	290 @ 5,800 rpm	290 lb-ft @ 4,200
L30	327 ci	275 @ 4,800 rpm	355 lb-ft @ 3,200
L48	350 ci	295 @ 4,800 rpm	380 lb-ft @ 3,200
L35	396 ci	325 @ 4,800 rpm	410 lb-ft @ 3,200
L78	396 ci	375 @ 5,600 rpm	415 lb-ft @ 3,600
1968			
Z28	302 ci	290 @ 5,800 rpm	290 lb-ft @ 4,200
L30	327 ci	275 @ 4,800 rpm	355 lb-ft @ 3,200
L48	350 ci	295 @ 4,800 rpm	380 lb-ft @ 3,200
L35	396 ci	325 @ 4,800 rpm	410 lb-ft @ 3,200
L34	396 ci	350 @ 5,200 rpm	415 lb-ft @ 3,400
L78	396 ci	375 @ 5,600 rpm	415 lb-ft @ 3,600
L89*	396 ci	375 @ 5,600 rpm	415 lb-ft @ 3,600

* Aluminum head 396

Year	Displacement	Horsepower	Torque
1969			
Z28	302 ci	290 @ 5,800 rpm	290 lb-ft @ 4,200
L48	350 ci	300 @ 4,800 rpm	380 lb-ft @ 3,200
L35	396 ci	325 @ 4,800 rpm	410 lb-ft @ 3,200
L34	396 ci	350 @ 5,200 rpm	415 lb-ft @ 3,400
L78	396 ci	375 @ 5,600 rpm	415 lb-ft @ 3,600
L89*	396 ci	375 @ 5,600 rpm	415 lb-ft @ 3,600
L72	427 ci +	425 @ 5,600 rpm	460 lb-ft @ 4,000
ZL1	427 ci +	430 @ 5,200 rpm	450 lb-ft @ 4,400

*Aluminum head 396
+COPO only

Year	Displacement	Horsepower	Torque
1970			
L48	350 ci	300 @ 4,800 rpm	380 lb-ft @ 3,200
Z28	350 ci	360 @ 5,800 rpm	370 lb-ft @ 4,000
L34	396 (402 ci)	350 @ 5,200 rpm	415 lb-ft @ 3,400
L78	396 (402 ci)	375 @ 5,600 rpm	415 lb-ft @ 3,600

Year	Displacement	Horsepower	Torque
1971			
L48	350 ci	270 @ 4,400 rpm	360 lb-ft @ 3,200
Z28	350 ci	330 @ 5,600 rpm	360 lb-ft @ 4,000
LS3	396 (402 ci)	300 @ 4,400 rpm	400 lb-ft @ 3,200
1972			
L48	350 ci	200 @ 4,400 rpm	300 lb-ft @ 2,800
Z28	350 ci	255 @ 5,600 rpm	280 lb-ft @ 4,000
LS3	396 (402 ci)	240 @ 4,400 rpm	345 lb-ft @ 3,200
1973			
L48	350 ci	175 @ 4,000 rpm	260 lb-ft @ 2,800
Z28	350 ci	245 @ 5,200 rpm	280 lb-ft @ 4,000
1974			
L48	350 ci	185 @ 4,000 rpm	270 lb-ft @ 2,600
Z28	350 ci	245 @ 5,200 rpm	280 lb-ft @ 4,000
1975			
L48	350 ci	155 @ 3,800 rpm	250 lb-ft @ 2,400
1976			
LM1	350 ci	165 @ 3,800 rpm	260 lb-ft @ 2,400
1977 1/2 Z28			
LM1	350 ci (160 hp California)	170 hp @ 3,800 rpm	270 lb-ft @ 2,400
1978 Z28			
LM1	350 ci (175 hp California)	185 hp @ 4,000 rpm	280 lb-ft @ 2,400
1979 Z28			
LM1	350 ci (170 hp California)	175 hp @ 4,000 rpm	270 lb-ft @ 2,400
1980 Z28			
LM1	350 ci (305 ci, 155 hp California)	190 hp @ 4,200 rpm	280 lb-ft @ 2,400
1981 Z28			
LG4	305 ci	165 hp @ 4,000 rpm	245 lb-ft @ 2,400
LM1	350 ci	175 hp @ 4,000 rpm	275 lb-ft @ 2,400
1982 Z28			
LG4	305 ci	145 hp @ 4,000 rpm	240 lb-ft @ 2,000
LU5	305 ci TBI	165 hp @ 4,200 rpm	240 lb-ft @ 2,400
1983 Z28			
LG4	305 ci	150 hp @ 4,000 rpm	240 lb-ft @ 2,400
LU5	305 ci TBI	175 hp @ 4,200 rpm	250 lb-ft @ 2,800
L69	305 ci H.O.	190 hp @ 4,800 rpm	240 lb-ft @ 3,200
1984 Z28			
LG4	305 ci	150 hp @ 4,000 rpm	240 lb-ft @ 3,200
L69	305 ci	190 hp @ 4,800 rpm	240 lb-ft @ 3,200

Year	Displacement	Horsepower	Torque
1985 Z28 and IROC Z28			
LG4	305 ci	155 hp @ 4,200 rpm	245 lb-ft @ 2,000
L69	305 ci	190 hp @ 4,800 rpm	240 lb-ft @ 3,200
LB9	305 ci	215 hp @ 4,400 rpm	275 lb-ft @ 3,200
1986 Z28			
LG4	305 ci	155 hp @ 4,200 rpm	245 lb-ft @ 2,000
LB9	305 ci	190 hp @ 4,800 rpm	240 lb-ft @ 3,200
L69	305 ci TPI	190 hp @ 4,000 rpm	285 lb-ft @ 2,800
1987 Z28 and IROC-Z			
LG4	305 ci	165 hp @ 4,400 rpm	245 lb-ft @ 2,800
LB9	305 ci (auto)	190 hp @ 4,000 rpm	295 lb-ft @ 2,900
LB9	305 ci (man.)	215 hp @ 4,400 rpm	250 lb-ft @ 3,200
B2L	350 ci	225 hp @ 4,400 rpm	330 lb-ft @ 2,800
1988 IROC-Z			
LO3	305 ci	170 hp @ 4,000 rpm	255 lb-ft @ 2,400
LB9	305 ci (auto)	195 hp @ 4,400 rpm	290 lb-ft @ 3,200
LB9	305 ci (man.)	220 hp @ 4,400 rpm	290 lb-ft @ 3,200
B2L	350 ci	230 hp @ 4,400 rpm	330 lb-ft @ 3,200
1989 RS and IROC-Z			
LO3	305 ci	170 hp @ 4,000 rpm	255 lb-ft @ 2,400
LB9	305 ci (auto)	195 hp @ 4,400 rpm	295 lb-ft @ 2,800
LB9	305 ci (man.)	220 hp @ 4,400 rpm	290 lb-ft @ 3,200
B2L	350 ci	230 hp @ 4,400 rpm	330 lb-ft @ 3,200
1990 RS and IROC-Z			
LO3	305 ci	170 hp @ 4,000 rpm	255 lb-ft @ 2,400
LB9	305 ci	220 hp @ 4,400 rpm	290 lb-ft @ 3,200
G92	305 ci	230 hp @ 4,400 rpm	300 lb-ft @ 3,200
B2L	350 ci	230 hp @ 4,400 rpm	330 lb-ft @ 3,200
1991 RS and Z28			
LO3	305 ci	170 hp @ 4,000 rpm	255 lb-ft @ 2,400
LB9	305 ci	210 hp @ 4,400 rpm	290 lb-ft @ 2,400
G92	305 ci	230 hp @ 4,400 rpm	300 lb-ft @ 3,200
B2L	350 ci	245 hp @ 4,400 rpm	330 lb-ft @ 3,200
1992 RS and Z28			
LB9	305 ci	230 hp @ 4,400 rpm	300 lb-ft @ 3,200
B2L	350 ci	245 hp @ 4,000 rpm	345 lb-ft @ 3,200
1993 Z28			
LT1	350 ci	275 hp @ 5,000 rpm	325 lb-ft @ 2,400
1994 Z28			
LT1	350 ci	275 hp @ 5,000 rpm	325 lb-ft @ 2,000
1995 Z28			
LT1	350 ci	275 hp @ 5,000 rpm	325 lb-ft @ 2,000
1996 Z28 and SS			
LT1	350 ci	285 hp @ 5,200 rpm	325 lb-ft @ 2,400
R7T	350 ci (SS)	305 hp @ 5,500 rpm	325 lb-ft @ 2,400
R7T	350 ci (SS*)	310 hp @ 5,500 rpm	325 lb-ft @ 2,400

* SS LT1 with optional performance exhaust

Year	Displacement	Horsepower	Torque
1997 Z28 and SS			
LT1	350 ci	285 hp @ 5,200 rpm	325 lb-ft @ 2,400
R7T	350 ci (SS)	305 hp @ 5,500 rpm	325 lb-ft @ 2,400
R7T	350 ci (SS*)	310 hp @ 5,500 rpm	325 lb-ft @ 2,400

* SS LT1 with optional performance exhaust

Year	Displacement	Horsepower	Torque
1998 Z28 and SS			
LS1	5.7 liter	305 hp @ 5,200 rpm	335 lb-ft @ 4,000
LS1	5.7 liter (SS)	320 hp @ 5,200 rpm	345 lb-ft @ 4,400

Technical Breakdown, Significant High-Performance Camaros

1967 Z28
Wheelbase	108.1 in
Length	184.6 in
Width	72.5 in
Engine	302-ci V-8
Horsepower	290

1969 SS-396
Wheelbase	108 in
Length	186 in
Width	74 in
Engine	396-ci V-8
Horsepower	325, 350, and 375

1970 Z28
Wheelbase	108 in
Length	188 in
Width	74.4 in
Engine	350-ci V-8
Horsepower	360

1977 Z28
Wheelbase	108 in
Length	195.4 in
Width	74.4 in
Engine	350-ci V-8 (5.7 liter)
Horsepower	170 (net)

1982 Z28
Wheelbase	101 in
Length	187.8 in
Width	72 in
Engine	305 ci V-8 (5.0 liter)
Horsepower	145 or 165 (net)

1985 IROC
Wheelbase	101 in
Length	187.8 in
Width	72 in
Engine	305-ci V-8 (5.0 liter)
Horsepower	190 or 215

1993 Z28
Wheelbase	101.1 in
Length	193.2 in
Width	74.1 in
Engine	350-ci V-8 (5.7 liter)
Horsepower	275

1998 Z28 SS
Wheelbase	101.1 in
Length	193.5 in
Width	74.1 in
Engine	5.7-liter V-8 (LS1)
Horsepower	320

Index